T0065730

The Godfather of Silicon Valley

GARY RIVLIN

THE GODFATHER OF SILICON VALLEY

Ron Conway and the Fall of

the Dot-coms

NEW YORK

Library of Congress Cataloging-in-Publication Data is available

ISBN 978-0-8129-9163-5

Website Address: www.atrandom.com

146484122

TO MY MOTHER, NAOMI RIVLIN,
IN HONOR OF SEVENTY REMARKABLE YEARS,

AND IN LOVING MEMORY OF

MARVIN KRUMHOLZ

1920–2001

Contents

Prologue

The embossed invitation sent to one thousand of Ron Conway's closest friends promised that Dana Carvey and Warren Buffett would be among the special guests attending his upcoming May 2000 "Silicon Valley Flies into Summer" bash. Mysterious "other celebrities" were also advertised, and as a further enticement, Conway described two of the many items he would be auctioning off for charity: a round of golf with Tiger Woods and Arnold Schwarzenegger's custom-designed black Hummer. Most people no doubt just shook their heads and smiled when they read their invitation. Dana Carvey and Warren Buffett, Tiger and Arnold: it was just *so* Ron Conway. Everywhere around them were signs that a remarkable era was drawing to a close, but few doubted that this man the local gossip columnists occasionally referred to as "the godfather of Silicon Valley" would put on a star-studded party as outsize and unreal as the boom-time Valley itself.

Conway lives in Atherton, a genteel Silicon Valley enclave where homes routinely sell for $5 million and it's not uncommon for a house to list for a sales price of $20 million or more. The grid of lanes and ways in this town of 7,800 has no curbs or sidewalks, and the street signs are mini Washington Monuments featuring street names etched in stone. The Conways routinely throw shindigs for five hundred guests or more, so in the days leading up to the Carvey-Buffett party the family went through what by that time had become an accustomed pre-party routine. A small squadron of off-duty Atherton cops was hired to patrol the grounds and one of the three

Conway Sons was dispatched to slip flyers into mailboxes warning neighbors in advance about the approaching confab.

Conway likes to hire a live band to play at his bigger bashes, but on this spring night he hired two, one for the cocktail hour and another for dancing later in the evening. He also put several extra off-duty cops on the payroll, including a few lined up to work undercover. "The last thing I needed," Conway says, "was for something to happen to Buffett while he was on my property." That night, the street in front of Conway's home was clogged by wall-to-wall limousines, while the valets served the single-digit millionaires who pulled up in their BMW 325i's and Porsche Boxsters. One guest counted five Ferraris, two Lamborghinis, and a Rolls. In many ways Conway serves as a perfect specimen for understanding the Internet frenzy that gripped the Valley at the close of the last century. Considered from that perspective, the party was as much a wake as it was a celebration. Here, in the geographical and spiritual center of entrepreneurial Silicon Valley, the digerati gathered for what some would later describe as a final hurrah.

Conway is chunky and of average height, a florid man with an aquiline nose and small mouth. He wears steel-framed glasses, and his snow white hair always seems as perfectly clipped as a putting green at Pebble Beach. If you passed him on the street, you'd be more likely to peg him as a successful midwestern insurance salesman than as one of the two or three best-connected people in Silicon Valley. He has dazzling blue eyes and a refined, slightly effeminate tinge to his voice that serves to take the edge off an otherwise boisterous and loud personality. On that night of the party in the portentous spring of 2000, Conway was forty-nine years old, though he looked much older.

The night before the party Conway spent hours reviewing his guest list. He was disappointed that many of the Valley's A-list stars had sent their regrets. He didn't really know Oracle's Larry Ellison, then the world's second-richest man, or Apple's Steve Jobs, or Linus Torvalds, the only man in Silicon Valley widely believed to be capable of walking on water. But Conway has always lived by the credo that it can't hurt to ask. Besides, plenty of the Valley's brightest lights had RSVP'd in the affirmative. The Internet's first boy wonder, Marc Andreessen, would be there, as would its newest, the nineteen-year-old founder of Napster, Shawn Fanning. So were a respectable number of the Valley's true royalty, the venture capitalists who wrote the multimillion-dollar checks Internet companies used to fund their explosive growth, and the investment bankers who took them public.

Conway pored over his guest list to remind himself which entrepreneurs he needed to introduce to which money men. He wrote the names out on lists that a couple of assistants carried with them all night so that they could periodically huddle with Conway to determine what corner of yard he still had to work. The idea of the party was to have fun, but fun for Conway means drinking and joking and tending to his guests while conducting business. "In any environment he's in," says former Netscape executive Jennifer Bailey, "Ron is multitasking, even if it's at his own party." At that point, Conway owned a small piece of roughly 240 Internet companies, and he had enlisted more than five hundred people as co-investors, including the big-dollar young brains behind companies such as Netscape and eBay, and a sprinkling of the famous and fabulous, from Shaq to Tiger to Henry Kissinger and Estée Lauder's grandkid Gary. There would be plenty of business to which to attend.

Attending a Conway party was like walking into a Dockers ad. There were square-jawed Stanford MBAs everywhere, wearing khakis, polos, and button-down shirts. It was a party to which people tended to arrive on time. After you gave your keys to some kid who seemed too young to drive, Conway, dressed casually in an open-collar dress shirt and no sports coat, would greet you as if you were a long-lost friend. He'd scan the immediate vicinity to see if there were any introductions to be made and if not he'd ask, "Would you like your picture taken with Warren?" You'd look to where Conway was gesturing and though you knew he'd be there it would be startling to encounter Buffett, gray eyebrows spiking like an overgrown crocus bed, dressed in a sensible tweed sports coat and wearing one of those "Hi my name is" stick-on badges. A picture with Warren—it was pure Conway, arranging it so you won't have to ask, bagging for you that most valuable of party favors, a choice head to mount on your own personal bragging wall.

Conway's rambling one-story ranch-style home is of a type most old-time Athertonians owned, before the area's new princes and princesses started knocking them down to build two- and three-story trophy homes heavy on columns and colonnades and fronted by grand plantation-style driveways. Conway and his wife, Gayle, had added an enormous, A-shaped brick façade entranceway to their house, but almost everyone who visited remarked on how modest a home it was. Visitors also tended to marvel at the backyard, a one-acre plot featuring a magnificent stand of soaring old-growth redwood trees, the perfect backdrop for a party for five hundred. In one corner, the raised front deck of a guesthouse served as a stage for the musicians and for Dana Carvey and Warren Buffett when they took the microphone. Waiters passed hors d'oeuvres prepared by Paula LeDuc: small pouches filled with caviar called Beggar's Purses and scallops wrapped in pancetta. A steel-drum band played and as the sun was setting tiki-torch lamps were lit.

Buffett took the stage at around eight-thirty. The party had been billed as a charity fund-raiser, but that was only partially true. Buffett certainly hadn't dragged his sixty-nine-year-old behind two thousand miles cross-country to help a bunch of rich Internet moguls raise a million or two for charity. He was there to pitch NetJets, a business owned by his holding company, Berkshire Hathaway. Think of NetJets as a kind of time-share for the fabulously well-to-do, a company that sells fractional jet ownership to both corporations and individuals. The head of NetJets, Richard Santulli, is one of Conway's 550 co-investors, and when the two were chatting a few months earlier, Santulli had fantasized out loud about pitching his services to a roomful of his fellow investors. Conway was a fan of the company and occasional customer, but he wasn't about to host a party so Santulli could sell shares in private executive jets. When he suggested that maybe NetJets could co-sponsor a charity event, Santulli offered to enlist Buffett in the cause. That's all Conway needed to hear. "If you get Warren Buffett to come," he told his friend, "I'll guarantee I'll do it. I'll also guarantee a big enough audience to produce a lot of visibility for NetJets."

The charity element of the event may have been incidental to Buffett, but it was important to Conway, who was always displeased when he read press accounts taking the Valley's youngest lords to task for their general lack of charitable giving. Conway had poured a staggering amount of money—and time—into a variety of charities, and he was intent on demonstrating how generous Silicon Valley can be. So when Schwarzenegger's people suggested Arnold would like to showcase his philanthropic side, Conway invited a half-dozen reporters to observe the event.

Buffett made his pitch and answered some questions, but the real fun began when Dana Carvey followed him up onstage to serve as the night's auctioneer. "Okay, you Silicon Valley billionaires," he began, and the next half hour could serve as archive footage that captured a magical moment in time.

The bidding started slowly. A magazine in which Conway was an early investor, *Red Herring,* donated a full-page four-color ad valued at $30,000, and threw in lunch with its editor, yet the high bid hit only $27,000; Conway bought a one-hour lesson with tennis great Pete Sampras for his wife (a round-trip seat on a NetJet Gulfstream IV included) for $40,000. A video featuring highlights of Shaquille O'Neal served as a prelude to the package that the basketball superstar had donated to the cause. Conway, who shared the podium with Carvey, called it the "Shaq package": four choice seats to a Lakers game, the promise of a meeting with O'Neal, and of course round-trip transportation courtesy of NetJets. Marc Andreessen won the bidding at $100,000. When Shaq's agent, who was in the crowd that night, threw in a second Shaq pack for the woman who had lost with a bid of $95,000, the crowd cheered as if witnessing a thunderous slam dunk. The bidding on a mystery box started at $5,000 and topped out at $20,000. Inside was a size-22 sneaker that Shaq had signed. Meanwhile, a dozen or so cheerleaders from the San Francisco 49ers cheering squad, dressed in their midriff-revealing outfits, shook their pom-poms and squealed. Finally it was time to auction the Schwarzenegger Hummer. The invitation had advertised that the winner would get a free one-way NetJets ride to LA for lunch with "Ahhhnuld" and to pick up the car, but then Conway had a brainstorm: he would display the car in his driveway for all his guests to view and thereby drive up the bidding. So all that week one of Conway's assistants was on the phone with one or another of Schwarzenegger's people, first trying to track down the car and then searching out the right people to sign the various releases and other authorizations. The next challenge was finding a towing company to haul this three-ton vehicle five hundred miles north to Atherton—on one day's notice. Conway had a special sign made up so that people would know that the gleaming black beast sitting by the entrance to his home had been custom-designed for Schwarzenegger and affectionately dubbed "The Terminator."

The Hummer bidding was also preceded by a videotape. Conway had asked Schwarzenegger's agent for maybe a few clips of his client's best-known movie scenes, but Schwarzenegger's crew did him one better, shooting a film of Arnold getting in and out of the Hummer and praising it as one of the jewels in his fleet. Appropriately, one of the Valley's matinee idols, Marc Andreessen, won the bidding at $140,000.

The evening's big prize was to be a foursome with Tiger Woods. The bidding opened at $250,000 and laddered up in $25,000 increments. As prearranged, partway through the bidding Buffett egged the crowd on by volunteering to serve as the group's caddy and then offer a stock tip at the eighteenth hole. Bids of $400,000, $500,000, $600,000: finally, Network Appliance's Tom Mendoza emerged as the top bidder at $650,000.

After the auction, people danced by tiki light while the real business of the evening was conducted. New Silicon Valley made connections with the old, the recently knighted royalty mingled with the area's princes-in-waiting, and clots of junior moguls gathered to talk deals and potential partnerships. Meanwhile, Conway, host to that grandest of all parties, Silicon Valley during the Internet boom, mingled among them, working his list. He drank, he roared with laughter, his complexion grew redder with each passing hour, but mainly he lovingly tended to his network, at once powerful and fragile, micromanaging every node of this living organism composed of his vast collection of colleagues, acquaintances, business partners, and friends. "How ya been?" he'd ask someone with a hearty pat on the back. "Can I get you a drink—oh, and have you met Joe, the CEO of that really hot search company I was telling you about?" He pushed, but not too hard. He'd flatter and he'd joke, and he'd talk and talk and talk. He is the perpetual salesman but a salesman with a patina of panache and class, an amiable and likable fellow who only wants to be everyone's best friend.

Later, Conway would declare the party a terrific success. He had sipped some fine Chardonnay, he talked shop with people he considered his friends, and he helped a portion of his 240 babies get one step closer to their mutual dreams of fabulous riches. What could be more fun than that?

—

It was in December 1998, at the height of the dot-com boom, that Ron Conway started contacting the friends he had collected over the years to ask them about investing in a fund he was calling Angel Investors; he raised $30 million in two months. By mid-1999, the rapid treadmill pace of business that had defined the Valley in the previous few years had sped up, as if the setting had changed from frenetic to frenzied. Every other office between San Jose and San Francisco, so it seemed, was now home for four whiz kids with a bang-up business plan hatched to tap some heretofore unknown billion-dollar market. Fat payoffs seemed as easy as picking low-hanging fruit, at least for those with the money and the moxie to cash in on what some were describing as a modern-day industrial revolution. It all seemed too much to pass up, and by summer's end Conway decided to create Angel Investors-II. This time he pulled every string within reach to put together a syndicate of Internetnavvy Investors with the connections and pull that would mean access to the best deals. Hollywood, he figured, could help foster the pending marriage between multimedia and the Internet, so he trolled for money there as well. "Anyone could have raised money in that environment," Conway says of Los Angeles. This was in the fall of 1999, when even the likes of William Shatner had made millions lending his name to Priceline.com in exchange for stock. "I could have raised five billion dollars in ten days," Conway says. That was obvious hyperbole, but he also had a point: the pickings were easy when every other celebrity in America was suddenly dreaming of being the next Shatner. Conway closed the fund just as 1999 was coming to a close, deciding to cap it at $150 million.

How easy was it to raise money during the last days of the Internet bubble? A few months after Conway's party, he was in the south of France, ensconced aboard a rented 151-foot yacht anchored off the Côte d'Azur—"one of those yachts," says Margot Hirsch, a longtime friend, "where when you see it you go, 'I wonder who's staying on *that?*' " Consequently, Hirsch dubbed her five days as part of Conway's entourage "Lifestyles of the Rich and Ron." Conway ventured into town one day to visit the opulent Hotel du Cap, where the likes of superagent Michael Ovitz (who tried to get into Conway's fund only after it was too late) and Steven Spielberg stay when they find themselves on the French Riviera. Conway was strolling the lobby with a high-profile Hollywood agent when they spotted Goldie Hawn, so they walked over to say hello. The animated Hawn only had to hear Conway's name. "Ron Conway?" she shrieked. "I've been looking all over Europe for you!" Hawn, it turns out, was in the early stages of an Internet-related startup of her own, and someone had told her that Conway was someone she needed to meet. Her money man had told her that Conway would also be vacationing in Europe, so apparently every time she checked into a hotel she asked if there was a Ron Conway staying there. The next day, Hawn joined the Conways for lunch on the yacht. A couple of months later, she'd attend Conway's next big party with her beau, Kurt Russell, and also Matt Damon and Ben Affleck, who had convinced Conway to invest in the Internet company that *they* had started.

The Hawn story goes a long way in explaining what *Newsweek* dubbed "The Whine of '99": "Everyone's getting rich but me!" The entire world, or so it seemed, wanted to own at least a small piece of the Internet fantasy, a dreamscape that produced a seemingly endless pool of boy billionaires. For those with the right connections and enough ready cash Conway offered the perfect investment vehicle.

Angel-I and Angel-II were like index funds of Internet startups, a way of owning a small piece of anything that was hot and trendy over the last couple of years of the decade. When the smart guys changed their minds, in late 1999, and declared that so-called "business-to-business" startups, and not the business-to-consumer dot-coms, were where the money was at, it didn't make a difference to Conway: he had invested in forty consumer sites and another forty sites geared to the business market. Angel Investors sunk several million dollars into Marc Andreessen's encore performance as an entrepreneur, Loudcloud, and it served as the first outside money in Napster. It owned a piece of Google, which *The New Yorker* had aptly described as "the default search engine for the in-crowd," and also Backflip, which could have been described using similar terms.

Wireless startups; incubators that nurtured a veritable rat's warren of tiny startups; infrastructure companies; next-generation search engine companies: whatever the hot trend of the moment, if you were a Conway investor, you owned a piece of it. In less than fifteen months' time, Conway and a couple of partners raced around the Valley slapping down bets as fast as they could, paying whatever it took whenever they discovered a promising company, because back then, at least, price didn't seem to matter. As the Internet continued to grow, so, too, would the net worth of the portfolio.

That at least was the theory.

The Godfather of Silicon Valley

Chapter 1

—

KING OF THE ANGELS

The Nasdaq was far from the top of its historic ascent the first time I heard Ron Conway's name. The locale was San Francisco, inside a Mission District café whose purveyor had only recently shared with me a stock tip. The particular Internet stock he mentioned didn't seem nearly as significant as the fact that he was whispering a stock at all. The moment called to mind Joe Kennedy's famous quip that he knew it was time to get out of the market when his shoeshine boy started giving him investment advice. In today's San Francisco the equivalent is the barista in a coffee bar sharing intelligence he overhears while jerking lattes.

My companion that morning was a neighbor and Internet entrepreneur, Andrew Beebe. Beebe was representative of a type one bumped into a lot, especially in 1999: jittery smart man-child CEOs, confident and bright, young men in their twenties who all seemed to know one another and one another's business. Beebe, twenty-eight, was the CEO of Bigstep, an Internet startup created to help mom-and-pop businesses get on the Internet. We were talking industry talk in an off-the-record kind of way when something I said spurred him to excitcatly boot up his laptop. He wanted to show off TheBrain, a software product that he only half-jokingly claimed had changed his life.

TheBrain allows users to render connections visually by linking and cross-linking anything residing on a computer hard drive— e-mails, random notes, an address. "The wonder of the mind and the source of human creativity," TheBrain's user guide tells us, "is the connectedness of all thoughts." Beebe, however, had employed the technology for a far more prosaic endeavor. Like the congressman who is already raising cash for his next run the morning after he is elected, the dedicated Valley entrepreneur was already raising his next round of financing while still buzzed on the adrenaline of that week's $15 million round. Beebe had harnessed TheBrain to help him make contact among the big-time venture capitalists on Sand Hill Road, the address of choice among the brand-name VCs. He had plugged in every A-list VC, and then linked them to anyone he knew with even a thread of connection to that name.

Think of TheBrain as a perfect way of visually rendering one's own personal Six Degrees of Separation. Beebe zoomed in to a random name and showed me the various connections he had to that VC. He pulled out to show me the macro view, and the screen vaguely resembled a road map of France. Thin squiggly lines ran everywhere. Occasionally there'd be a slight thickening around, say, Lyon or Marseilles, but then near Paris the lines came together into an indistinguishable lump. TheBrain, it seemed, was suffering from a life-threatening ganglion cyst. Beebe zoomed in to the center of the mass. As in France, where all roads lead to Paris, within the money-raising world all roads led to this man Beebe called "the king of the angels."

———

The use of the term "angel" in a business context dates back to the start of the last century, when it was used on Broadway to flatter wealthy benefactors willing to pony up the capital required to stage a theater production. Nowadays the term, at least in less celestial discussions, is most often used to refer to rich individuals who invest in fledgling technology companies. Apple Computer was started with angel funding, as were Amazon.com and a long list of profitless, no-name companies that nonetheless went public and returned an imponderable payout for their patron saints.

"The grassroots of American capitalism have never been better watered," *U.S. News* declared in 1997 in a lengthy feature article about the angel phenomenon. According to the University of New Hampshire's Center for Venture Research, an estimated 250,000 active angel investors sank a staggering $20 billion into small companies. By 1999, those figures would swell to 400,000 angels investing an estimated $30 billion. The money flowing into venture capital funds was more staggering still. "At the height of the Internet frenzy," says Jeff Bonforte, founder of a company called I-drive.com, "friends of your friends' dads were begging to give you money." At the same time, entrepreneurs such as Bonforte were all competing for the same small group of platinum, well-connected investors, especially those widely regarded as the industry's top-tier venture capitalists.

In 1997, Paul Saffo, a director at the Menlo Park–based Institute for the Future and one of the area's better-known pundits, told me that there was so much money pouring into the Valley that "there aren't enough rat holes to put it down." That year venture firms invested a record $14 billion dollars in startups, according to the National Venture Capital Association (NVCA) and Venture Economics—a fivefold increase over the venture dollars invested just six years earlier. Yet even that record-shattering figure was soon to be dwarfed. VCs invested more than $15 billion in startups in the last three months of 1999 alone, and in the year 2000 venture investments topped $100 billion for the year. College endowments, employee pension funds, foundations, rich individuals: as a group, each dramatically upped the percentage of its holdings earmarked for these highest of high-risk investment vehicles. And why not? In 1994, the venture firm Sequoia Capital had invested $2 million in Yahoo; by 1999, assuming Sequoia and its investors hadn't sold a single share, its Yahoo stake would be worth more than $4 billion. The $6.7 million Benchmark invested in eBay in

1997 was worth $400 million when the company went public in September 1998, just nineteen months later, and an incredible $4 billion by the following spring. By 1999, the average Sand Hill Road venture capital firm specializing in early-stage investments was providing returns of 47 percent a year over the previous five years, according to the NVCA and Venture Economics. The most successful houses, such as Benchmark and Sequoia, were spinning out returns exceeding 100 percent per year.

Money of every kind rained down on Silicon Valley in the second half of the 1990s. There was the venture community's so-called "smart" money, which came with connections and presumably the collective wisdom of the firm's partners, and also "dumb" money, from rich people who knew nothing about the Internet except that it seemed to be a money tree for those well connected enough to get in early. Money poured in from Japan and Europe, money flowed from the scores of established corporations, ranging from Intel and Hewlett-Packard to Citibank, that had created corporate venture divisions. Where in 1995 corporate venture investments totaled $177 million, according to the NVCA and Venture Economics, in 1999 that figure had grown by a factor of 44, to nearly $8 billion.

Everyone with the means wanted to play. In early 1999, two former members of the San Francisco 49ers football team, Ronnie Lott and Harris Barton, created Champion Ventures, a venture fund for professional athletes. In less than two years, the pair raised $190 million from 250 athletes, both active and retired, whose money would piggyback on the investments made by some of the Valley's most successful venture firms. Companies such as OffRoad Capital, established in 1999, were created to help America's latest disadvantaged group—the very rich shut out of private investment opportunities ("At OffRoad Capital, we simply won't rest until we give this country's excluded millionaires the pre-public investment access they so rightfully deserve"). The meVC Draper Fisher Jurvetson Fund became the first publicly traded venture capital stock when it debuted on the New York Stock Exchange in June 2000. Even the CIA jumped into the game with In-Q-Tel, a $28 million pot of cash set aside to help fund startups that might augur improvements in the spy business.

With all that money floating around it was no surprise that the Valley startup scene was hit with the kind of inflation usually witnessed in troubled Third World countries. A one-quarter share in an early-stage startup that would have cost a VC maybe $1 million back in 1995 cost between $5 million and $8 million by 1999, if not more if the founders were a known quantity. Later rounds swelled proportionately. Venture capitalists talk about a seed round, or A round, and then letter subsequent rounds accordingly. Twenty-seven-year-old MBAs running six-month-old startups were routinely raising $20 to $30 million in B and C rounds of financing. What percentage of a company the investors would in turn own depended on the "post-money" valuation, which is Valleyspeak for the paper worth of a company after a round of funding is completed, as agreed upon by the company's stakeholders. In 1995, a venture capital firm throwing $4 million into the pot as part of a B-round financing would have secured a 20 percent stake in the company, assuming a then-typical post-money valuation of $20 million. By the end of the decade, though, the new economy would price that same company at $100 million. So the $4 million investment that bought 20 percent of a company in 1995 now bought only 4 percent. Even at those prices the competition was stiff, and even well-regarded VCs were routinely cutting corners when conducting due diligence for fear of being locked out of a deal.

Inflation meant technology startups had money to burn, and they tended to do just that, like the ten-month-old Silicon Valley consulting firm that offered a free $40,000 Mercedes sports car to any employee who referred a new employee. Companies spent lavishly on everything from $2,000 office chairs to free daily lunches for employees to the $3 million several dot-coms paid for thirty seconds during the Super Bowl. Inflation also meant that most VCs wouldn't even look at a deal for anything less than a few million dollars, and angel investors accordingly assumed a more central role in the Valley's economic ecosystem.

In the fall of 1998, Artie Wu, the co-founder of a company called Vividence, found himself sitting in the offices of Kleiner Perkins Caufield & Byers, the most envied and sought-after venture firm on Sand Hill Road. At that point Wu and his co-founder were just two guys working out of Wu's apartment on what they hoped was a winning idea for an Internet business. Kleiner partner Russ Siegelman was impressed—until the two talked money. With time, Siegelman would prove open to six-figure seed rounds, but back then he was new enough as a VC and uncertain enough of the potential payoff of Wu's idea that he proved reluctant to take the idea to his partners. Wu, it turns out, didn't need nearly enough to satisfy Kleiner's usual appetite.

"How much do you need?" Siegelman asked.

"Five hundred thousand dollars."

As Wu told it, Siegelman did a double take. "You mean five million?" he quotes Siegelman as saying. (Siegelman, for his part, couldn't recall much about the conversation.) When Wu repeated the figure he had in mind, Siegelman gave Wu several names, including Conway's. That's how Wu became one of the first entrepreneurs to be funded by Angel Investors. Until that point, Wu had never heard of Conway, yet now he describes him as "the very first person I'd call if starting another company."

Wu is inclined to view the typical angel as an individual who invests in a few startups on the hopes one hits it big so he has something to boast about at cocktail parties. By contrast, Wu describes Conway as one of the ten or twenty most important people in Silicon Valley. "Ron is one of those core engines that make the Valley run," says Wu, whose company has gone on to win rave reviews from the trade press. "Sure, the rest of us are on the playing field, but we're just playing our small roles while these guys are like the turbines that make everything go."

———

That Wu had never heard of Conway is not surprising. A Nexis search conducted in the spring of 2000 revealed that Conway didn't cut nearly as high a profile as the companies he backed. There was a single appearance on CNN, a couple of mentions in *The New York Times,* the occasional quote in one of the big general-interest business magazines, and beyond that little except a mention every month or two in the *San Francisco Chronicle* or *San Jose Mercury News.* There were more hits for articles quoting a railroad executive with the same name. Donna Sokolsky, "Chief Firecracker" at Sparkpr, one of the more sought-after PR agencies among Valley startups, dubs Conway "the Valley's best-kept secret." Conway is not particularly secretive, but neither is he publicity hungry. For a time Sokolsky's firm handled publicity for Conway, but rarely did he want them to do anything for him beyond handling calls from reporters seeking an interview, and there weren't many of those. Mention Conway to even seasoned business reporters and the odds are good that they'll say, Ron who?

But to Valley insiders, Conway was legendary. "He's the archangel," says the Institute for the Future's Paul Saffo. "It's gotten to the point where if you say 'angel,' people think 'Conway.' " Saffo, who has lived and worked in the Valley for the better part of twenty years, adds, "I don't think I've ever met someone who doesn't know Ron."

There are better-known angel investors than Conway. Charles Schwab is an angel, as are Sanford Robertson of Robertson Stephens fame and AOL's Steve Case. Yet stacked up side by side with Conway they are mere hobbyists, dilettantes invited into deals for no other reason than their sizable stash of cash and the cachet their name would lend a project. Other angels have had far more lucrative payouts than Conway has ever had, but Conway doesn't reign as the Valley's archangel because of his prowess for picking the hottest companies in which to invest. Conway's best pick to date is Ask Jeeves, and on that investment the return was maybe 5X, or five times his original investment. He ended up taking a round-trip on Jeeves, riding it to its peak of $174 and then riding it back down into the single digits before he sold any shares. That's Conway, in it for the money, but also a true believer who holds on to favorites for longer than is healthy for his bottom line.

"The analogy I like to use for Ron is he's like the Valley's baby nanny," says Donna Sokolsky. "Say you just had a baby. Would you want the thirteen-year-old kid next door baby-sitting your kid or would you want the baby nanny?"

—

As the ranks of the angels swelled, small groups banded together in informal networks. There was a social aspect to the phenomenon, but more practical reasons were the primary motivator: performing due diligence on a deal is that much quicker if you've assembled a group of people, each of whom brings a different expertise. The first organized effort that received any press attention was the Valley-based Band of Angels, a loose collection of former executives from top technology firms who have been gathering once a month since 1995. They meet at the Los Altos Golf and Country Club, where in a typical evening they will hear from the two or three entrepreneurs who've been invited to pitch by at least one Band member. Sports jackets and ties are mandatory among the men, and even the guest entrepreneurs are asked to pay $100 to defray the cost of dinner, though a Band member in good standing must have a net worth of at least $1 million—most, of course, are worth far more—and are expected to invest at least $50,000 a year in startups presenting to the group.

The Band caused a stir in 1998 when some of its more aggressive members convinced the startup Sendmail to accept their money instead of waiting for a top-tier VC firm that had expressed keen interest but was insisting on several weeks to conduct background checks and perform other basic due-diligence tasks. Until that point, the lines of demarcation between the VCs and angels had always been clear: the angels were like the farm system and the VCs the major leagues, and no entrepreneur in his right mind would play in a triple-A stadium if invited to play in San Francisco's Pacific Bell Park. The Band invested a combined $5 million in Sendmail. The renegade group of angels in the deal, it turns out, was led by Conway and a serial entrepreneur turned angel named Marc Porat.

The VCs grumbled that Conway & Co. paid too high a price for too small a share of the company. "The problem when amateurs play venture capitalist," says one longtime VC, "is they don't know how to price the deal, making it more expensive for everyone down the road." Conway, in turn, defended the premium they paid as the price of victory. Whatever the truth, now even amateurs, assuming they had the money and the brass to roll the dice in such spectacular fashion, were joining the hunt for the multimillion-dollar A- and B-round deals. In a world that was already going temporarily mad, the players would be in that much more of a hurry, driven by the growing influence of an entirely new set of players.

It can be said that an angel is nothing but a wanna-be VC playing with his or her own money. Yosi Amram lost one job as Internet CEO in part because his board believed he was spending too much time watching after his portfolio of angel investments, yet in his next CEO posting he would continue working with fledgling companies in which he had invested. "Deep within Yosi Amram," wrote a reporter for the trade publication *Inter@ctive Week,* "beats the heart of a venture capitalist." It's no wonder. By the mid-1990s, the VCs had taken center stage, supplanting the leveraged buyout artists. A Stanford professor named Joseph Grundfest even compared them to the Medicis. Rare was the successful Silicon Valley executive who didn't secretly hold out hope that one day Kleiner Perkins, impressed with their picking prowess as angel, would offer them a job as a general partner.

Yet Conway was no longer a wanna-be, at least once he had created Angel Investors. In most every way the king of the angels actually resembles a classic venture capitalist. Like any VC, he plays mainly with other people's money, not his own. He charges an annual management fee, which pays for expenses, such as the salary he pays himself and also a couple of fellow partners and a support staff, and he will profit handsomely if the fund does well, like any partner in any venture firm. VCs call it "the carry," the 20 to 30 percent a firm's general partners skim off the top before disbursing any profits. (For instance, Benchmark Capital's five partners split evenly among themselves a 30 percent share of the roughly $4 billion the firm made on its eBay investment, or more than $200 million each, before apportioning the remaining shares to their firm's investors, known as limited partners.)

The 20 percent carry Conway charges is typical, but its 3 percent annual management fee is high because, Conway explains, "we anticipated that we'd have a much larger portfolio of companies than the typical VC." (He also notes that his deal dictates that he can charge "up to" 3 percent; unlike many VCs, who treat any leftover management fee money as an annual bonus, he takes only as much as Angel Investors needs to cover that year's expenses.) Angel Investors is formally structured like a traditional VC fund, according to the legal paperwork used to create the partnership, and despite its name, Angel Investors was often not the first money in a startup, or even the first outside money discounting a friends-and-family round. Often they invested in B and C rounds and occasionally a D round. In mid-1999, Angel Investors invested $250,000 in the A round of a multimedia infrastructure company called Dotcast, and then followed with $1 million in a B round later that year and another $1 million in a C round held in mid-2000. That's something else that distinguishes Conway from the typical angel: like the VCs, he does follow-on financing.

"A lot of people have impressive Rolodexes," says the venture capitalist Lise Buyer, an investor in Conway's fund, "but only Ron thought of using it to put together a fund like Angel Investors. He not only has the relationships to bring us all together, which very few people do, but also the patience and the personality." The strata reserved for the Valley's best-connected players doesn't include many salesmen, yet who but a master salesman could sell 550 investors, all of them high-powered in their own realm, on something like Angel Investors?

———

The Nasdaq had experienced its first huge convulsion by the time I contacted Conway in July 2000. It had fallen by another thousand points by the time he agreed to "squeeze" me in four months later for lunch the day before Thanksgiving. Conway arrived twenty minutes late behind the wheel of a black Mercedes. He was wearing a dress shirt and slacks and carried a heavy stack of papers under his arm. He may play baby nanny to more than two hundred fledgling Internet startups, but he doesn't own a laptop computer, a Palm, or geekware of any kind except a cell phone, which he is never without.

There is something immediately likable about this man whom you might peg as an insurance adjuster coming to check out the damage to your car. Those who fancy themselves Valley kingmakers are typically big, blustery types who enjoy throwing around their clout, yet that hardly describes Conway. He's almost pathologically polite. He apologized for being late to lunch and he apologized that he's been so hard to reach and he apologized that it had taken us four months to hook up, though he had already apologized for that over the phone.

I had decided that the best way to engage Conway was to take on the role of an entrepreneur selling him on both me and my idea. I wasn't seeking a few hundred thousand dollars for my startup but something far more precious: Conway's time. Despite the implied optimism of a brief e-mail he had sent to me in mid-2000 (repeated here in its entirety: "I'm sorry I'm too busy till end of the year. Ron"), 2001 was already shaping up to be as hectic a year as the then current one. At its peak, Angel Investors employed a staff of twelve, but often one of his portfolio CEOs or investors wanted to speak directly with him. When I suggested that I occasionally tag along as he went about his business and interview him in the car between appointments, it wasn't the intrusion on his daily business he minded but the intrusion on his downtime in the car, which is when he caught up on phone calls. "I'd lose my mind if what I was doing wasn't so interesting," he said offhandedly. Even the next day, Thanksgiving, was going to be something of a workday, as he anticipated "three or four hours of paperwork" sitting in front of the TV. That would be the calm before the pending storm. "The weekend is really going to be ugly," he said.

As is, he said he felt totally overcommitted. There was only so much time his scheduler could carve out so the two of us could meet for lunch. I proposed a cap on the hours I would spend interviewing him over the coming months; he said that might work. At that suggestion he looked more relieved than anything else. As a former salesman, he had spent too much of his adult life hating the word "no." It seemed as unpleasant for him to say the word as for him to hear it from someone else. All things considered, he'd much rather share in someone's excitement for an idea than throw cold water on it.

He wanted the long weekend to sit with the decision. Conway the salesman would understand why I didn't quite believe him. For one thing, three or four times he had spoken about when, not if. He had even counseled me on how he wanted me to approach his "superstar CEOs." ("I want you to tell them, 'Ron has sanctioned this project, he's welcomed me in, but he wants me to say that if you're superbusy, or if you're in a funding cycle, then Ron says you're not to do this.' ")

But mainly I knew he would say yes because of a gift he had handed me at the end of our time together. After my allotted hour, he had me accompany him to his car, where he retrieved from his trunk a thick book he had recently prepared for Angel Investors' annual meeting. Within its pages were the names of all 550 of his investors, and a company-by-company listing of every investment Conway had made, including the number of shares he had bought at what price. One page listed the precise dollar figure the fund had made (or lost) on each company going public, another spelled out that same set of figures for Angel startups that had been acquired by larger companies. As I sat on the curb outside the restaurant excitedly flipping through its pages, I realized I had sold him.

Chapter 2

—

DOUBLING DOWN

L ong before anyone might describe Conway as one of the turbines that make the Valley go, he was a guy frustrated that he
wasn't getting paid as well as he should. The year was 1979, and
he was working at National Semiconductor, his first job after college. He had moved quickly up the ladder at National Semi, from
research analyst to account executive to the director of the Santa
Clara–based chip manufacturer's automotive sales division. There
hadn't been much of an automotive division when Conway took
over, but that was precisely the point. By his third year in that post,
chip sales to car manufacturers accounted for roughly half the
company's earnings, and he thought he deserved a big raise.

Conway was earning $50,000 a year, a princely sum back then, es-
pecially for a twenty-eight-year-old with a liberal arts degree from
San Jose State, but in his mind his age was irrelevant. He demanded
that he be paid $100,000 a year and granted a sizable share of stock
options. When his boss told him no, Conway pulled out financials he
had prepared in advance of the meeting. Even then he was a relent-
less salesman who interpreted a "no" as nothing more than a verbal

clue that he needed to try a different tack. Conway pushed, prompting his boss to cut to the bottom line: There's no way we're going to pay a kid in his twenties a dime over fifty grand. That week Conway had received a call from someone who had left National Semi to work at a local startup stamping out plastic boxes that people were calling personal computers. Conway phoned his former colleague and proposed lunch. That's how Conway landed, at the dawn of the PC era, a job that would make him a millionaire many times over.

Conway knew next to nothing about the PC, but then he had never understood the first thing about the semiconductors he sold except that car manufacturers bought them by the truckload because they had no choice given the U.S. government's newly imposed emission control laws. What he understood about the PC is that the company offering him a top executive's job, Altos Computer Systems, was a nine-person operation that was earning a 50 percent pretax profit on every machine sold. He also understood that his salary as vice president of marketing meant he could afford to buy a much bigger house for his wife and growing family, and that the financial reward, if everyone who was part of the company played their cards right, was near limitless. Altos's founder, David Jackson, granted Conway a 1 percent stake in the company, but Conway lived by the credo that if you don't toot your own horn, no one else will, so he made sure to "rattle the cage every time I did something good." He would close a big sale and then walk into Jackson's office to demand more stock. By the time of Altos's stock market debut, in November of 1982, Conway owned 2 percent of the company, a stake worth more than $5 million the day it went public.

Conway's reputation inside Altos was that of someone who both worked and played hard. He had an ease about him that people generally found alluring, and though people would describe him as the consummate salesman, he was never a crude backslapper but instead the type who killed you through attention. "Ron was maybe the best salesman I've ever seen," says Bob Bozeman, a fellow Altos exec. "He would take the toughest guys, the ones that everyone thought would be impossible to sell. A guy who had hurdles all around him. Ron would take that as a personal challenge."

He was often on the road five days a week, and when people remember Conway then they recall him drinking a glass of wine at a hotel bar talking shop with a customer or underlings. At the close of the 1984 Comdex show, Conway gathered his sales force of about twenty at a French restaurant called Andre's to celebrate some long-forgotten sales milestone. They began by ordering Dom Pérignon, and when they had purchased Andre's entire stock of Dom they kept ordering champagne until they had bought every last bottle in the house, including a jeroboam-sized display bottle that makes a magnum look as if it's a thimble. The bill came to more than $5,000. "Ron was in his early thirties and seemed to be having the time of his life," says Margot Hirsch, a family friend. "He's a man who thrives on being the life of the party."

The party wouldn't last, however. By 1985, only three years after it had gone public, the company's once promising future seemed decidedly dreary, and Conway quit. "I saw that the market was getting ugly and that Altos was going downhill fast," Conway recalls. He spent the next few years throwing himself into philanthropy, mainly as a fundraiser for causes helping sick children, while serving as a consultant to a variety of Valley startups, always choosing equity in lieu of payment, given he had plenty of cash stashed away. That proved to be a lucrative decision. One of the companies was purchased by Microsoft, another by Adobe.

Conway's hiatus from the corporate world came to an end in 1988. As Conway tells it, a desperate David Jackson phoned Conway to try to lure him back to Altos. Realizing that it would be a lousy life flying the world to save a crumbling business, he demanded an additional 2 percent share of the company and what he describes as a "monstrous salary." Yet it was a third condition that proved too much for Jackson to endure. "I told him, 'And if I decide two weeks after I'm back that this piece of shit has to be sold, I have complete power to sell.' " Presented with that demand, Conway remembers, Jackson called him an asshole and hung up the phone. But then two weeks later Jackson phoned back and told him, "Get your ass in here." Within a few months of his return, the company's CEO was out and Conway took the reins (Jackson still served as company chairman). One of the first things Conway did was enlist the investment banking firm of Morgan Stanley to find a potential suitor to buy the company. Two grueling years later, in 1990, a Taiwan-based PC company bought Altos for $94 million, and Conway pocketed nearly $2 million on the sale. A few months after the acquisition, he was gone.

At that point Conway was thirty-nine years old. He contemplated a return to the more relaxed life of consulting and charity fundraising, but that was a fleeting thought for this man whom one friend describes as "one of the most driven human beings I've ever met." Anxious to be his own boss, he bought a majority stake in a computer training company called Personal Training Systems and took over as CEO. Later, he would remember a two-year tenure at the helm of PTS, but his résumé indicates he ran the company for more than half a decade. "If I was there that long, I was miserable," he says. Not long after buying PTS, he realized that he'd never grow the company into a $50 million a year business, as he had dreamed, but he was instead destined to be the CEO of a $5 million a year "shitty business" that he found neither interesting nor challenging.

Conway started looking for a buyer shortly after taking over PTS. That search proved even more frustrating than the Altos sale—but also more remunerative. When I asked Conway if he made any return on his investment, he answered in a matter-of-fact, you're-nuts-to-think-otherwise tone. "Oh yeah. Yeah. Yeah. That was very lucrative. All my stops have been lucrative." This time he had been extremely lucky. When finally he found an Irish-based buyer, CBT Systems, in early 1996, PTS was less than two months from shutting its doors due to a lack of revenues. Compounding his luck, shares in the publicly traded CBT were about to explode, and Conway had been paid with stock. His normally understated close friend Bill Campbell would call the sale a "terrific, terrific windfall."

Yet Conway had learned a hard lesson. He was tired of assuming commitments that stole him away from his family and then, perversely, required every ounce of his being to extract himself. His new plan was to dabble rather than dive into whatever came next. This was 1996 and the Valley was seeing an explosion of promising young companies in which he could invest and lend his expertise. At that point he couldn't say he understood the Internet, but clearly, whatever it was, it was a big deal.

—

It was Conway's good fortune to have grown up in the San Francisco Bay Area. If he had grown up in, say, Dayton, Ohio, he would no doubt have been successful, but he would more likely have been an executive at a Fortune 500 company, living well but not gloriously so. He lived in San Francisco until he was fifteen, when his father moved the family to Atherton. He got married in his early twenties, but he soon returned to this leafy enclave less than a ten-minute drive from Stanford. He had no real interest in computers—he refused to go on a sales call at Altos unless accompanied by a technician ("I refused to touch the machines," Conway says)—so he would have hardly been the type to have stampeded west with others seeking to cash in on their technological know-how in the mid-1990s. But living where he did, so close to ground zero in the Great Internet Land Rush set off when Netscape when public in August 1995, he couldn't help but feel the hum of opportunity vibrating in the air.

He was born in 1951, tied for sixth place (he is a twin) in a large Irish Catholic family of twelve children. His father was a top executive at the Oakland-based shipping giant American President Lines, until the senior Conway quit to cash in on the nascent container shipping business. He sold the resulting business in the mid-1960s, "for a couple of million dollars," Conway says, adding that "forty years ago that was a lot of money," as if it were a mere pittance today. That's how the family was able to move into a house in Atherton that recently went on the market priced at $18 million.

His twin, Rick, and oldest brother, John Jr., agree that their semi-famous brother takes after their dad, who died of a heart attack when he was only fifty-six. The family belonged to the semi-exclusive Olympic Club, where John Sr. organized "Irish Corner" parties; as all three brothers tell it, he had the same large blustery personality and the same propensity to both work and play hard. They cast the old man standing at a microphone at an Irish Corner party, face flushed from drink and lit up with pleasure. The family attended church every Sunday, and for a time the senior Conway was active in San Francisco politics, a strong Democratic enclave. That made it all the more surprising when his son Ron worked on Nixon's 1968 campaign, and then got actively involved in local Republican party politics. "My dad couldn't figure out where his sons got their Republican side," says Rick Conway, who describes both himself and his twin as dyed-in-the-wool conservatives. "He must have asked us a dozen times, 'Now, why are you for Nixon?' "

Ron Conway was shy as a child. "In grammar school," his twin brother stresses, "*no one* would have expected he'd become the mayor of Silicon Valley." He was never much of a student, which is how he ended up at a community college before transferring to San Jose State in his junior year, nor was he much of an athlete. Inside a family as large as his, where the oldest and youngest were born only fourteen years apart, the twelve of them were pretty much a self-contained unit. The transfer from an all-boys parochial school in the city to Menlo-Atherton High, a public high school, proved a pivotal moment in Conway's life. Maybe his truest self couldn't grow in the liberal soil of San Francisco, only taking hold in conservative Atherton. "It was in high school where I became more outspoken," Conway says.

Conway was still at Menlo-Atherton High when he met the wives of several POWs upset by the constant protests against the Vietnam War. To counteract the noisy student protesters at nearby Stanford, Conway helped organize a high school assembly in support of the POWs. At twenty-one years old he was elected to the Atherton City Council. Still living with his family while attending college, he ran on a two-plank platform in which he opposed the proposed widening of a major thoroughfare in an adjoining town and strongly favored a raise for the local police. "That was when Ron started building his network," John Conway says. He stepped down three years into his term because getting married meant he could no longer afford to live in the town he was representing.

Conway hasn't paid much attention to politics since that time. He contributed $50,000 to George W. Bush's 2000 presidential campaign, and flew east for the new president's inauguration, but he's hardly someone you would describe as politically engaged. Abortion? Gun control? "I could care less," he says about these and other ideological battles. In that way, he's the prototype Valleyite, so consumed by making money and success that he makes little time for anything else. He cares about the government, he says, to the extent it has an impact on the business climate. He's a voracious reader but hardly an intellectual, reading little except business and trade magazines, even while on vacation. One industry figure remembers running into Conway at the Four Seasons on Hawaii's Kohala Coast, a favorite getaway spot for the Valley's digerati. There was Conway sitting poolside, reading through a tall stack of trade magazines. He enjoys regular trips to Las Vegas, but doesn't gamble, and his frequent trips to Los Angeles are because his two oldest sons attend UCLA and he invariably has a long list of work reasons to be there.

It's not unusual for Conway to catch three or four industry parties in a week. For him there's his work, his wife and three sons, his pet charities, and little else. Peter Godfrey is an investor in Conway's fund, the founder of Micro Warehouse, and a friend. He's also a co-founder of *Maxim,* a slightly dressed-up *Playboy* based in LA and aimed at men under thirty. (A joke of the day from *Maxim*'s website: "Q: Why do men find it difficult to make eye contact? A: Breasts don't have eyes.") When *Maxim* held a huge bash to promote itself, the party was predictably Hugh Hefner in style, but Conway was apparently there to support a friend and investor—and of course do some business. "There's all these scantily clad women, and yet Ron goes to these parties to network," Margot Hirsch says. "He brought his son along and worked the entire time. He might be the only man I've ever met with no interest in looking at the girls."

—

Conway's angel career had begun even while he was stuck running Personal Training Systems. Conway was already meeting the budding entrepreneurs who would play a pivotal role in his new career, including a Sun Microsystems employee named Kim Polese. Polese was the marketing manager for Java, a new programming language developed within Sun and perfectly suited for the Internet, when Conway approached her to propose a business relationship between the two companies. Conway was impressed with how the thirty-three-year-old Polese handled herself. He viewed her as a bright young woman and mentally he marked her as a comer. So when he read in 1996 that Polese had left Sun, along with two other key members of the Java team, to start their own company (along with a fourth Java veteran who had left the company the previous year), he immediately tracked her down. He was not subtle. From their first conversation he made it clear that he wanted to invest in her company, and for well over a year he kept hammering at the point.

Wired magazine had shown up their first day in their new offices for a photo shoot. On their second day they were written up in *USA Today,* though they hadn't yet chosen their company name, Marimba. At a time when it seemed half the Valley was pretending to be Internet savvy, the Marimba team could boast of impeccable credentials: Polese and at least two of her partners could legitimately claim to have played a critical role in Java's success. Polese figures she heard from more than two dozen potential suitors in the company's earliest days, yet for the moment she and her three partners would live off their savings as they tried to figure a way to use Java to more efficiently distribute complex programs over the Internet. For the time being, she had more than enough incoming without this Conway character calling her all the time.

"He was incredibly persistent," says Polese, who didn't recall that the two had dealt with each other briefly while she was still at Sun. "I didn't know him. I didn't know the name."

At that point Conway had already invested in a few Internet companies and also the *Red Herring,* a magazine that focused on the venture capital field. He had only just recently learned of the Band of Angels, but as with most everything in his life, he threw himself into the group with the zeal of the true believer. A Band member was permitted to invite an entrepreneur to one of its monthly pitch meetings if he or she was already committed to investing in that company. Where the average member might bring one new company a year to the group, Conway was sponsoring a new startup each month. His appetite for new deals seemed insatiable.

Six months after they left Sun to great fanfare in the summer of 1996, the Marimba team announced that they had chosen the Valley's premier venture capital firm, Kleiner Perkins, to fund their first round. Kleiner's John Doerr, the venture world's one bona fide superstar, had invited Polese to lunch, the two had hit it off, and the deal was sealed. Conway was disappointed but not deterred. This was 1996, before inflation hit the startup world, so the $4 million Kleiner paid for a one-fifth interest in this company barely six months old was at once startling and confirmed what Conway knew: Marimba was a hot deal.

"My strategy was to do what I could to be a friend and an adviser to Kim, all the while reminding her, 'Hey, if I can ever get in, I'd like to get in,' " Conway recalls. He was a veteran whose perspective Polese appreciated, but she explained that an angel investor no longer made any sense when they already had venture capitalists and corporate partners lining up to do a next round.

Conway, however, was not an easy man to deter. Polese would show up at a cocktail party and there would be Conway walking over to say hello, a drink in hand, a broad smile on his face. She'd see him at industry events, she'd bump into him at work-related Christmas parties, she'd fly into Phoenix for the Agenda conference and there he'd be. Or she'd return from a business trip and among her phone messages would be two from Conway. She'd call him back in part because she was curious but also because there was a prospective customer angle that Conway proved adept at playing. At that point, Conway still did some work for the company that had purchased Personal Training Systems, and he was dangling the possibility of a training program to teach developers Marimba's technology. So he'd call Polese to talk about a training deal and then naturally he'd ask how she was doing. That was typical Conway, wearing two hats simultaneously, using one to help advance the purposes of the other.

"He was very pushy," Polese says, "but in an inoffensive way. In fact, in a rather charming way. That he cared about the human side was very clear. He was very skillful in the way that he was persistent."

Polese shocked even herself when, in September of 1997, she invited Conway to participate in Marimba's second round of financing, along with Kleiner and several larger corporations that could serve as strategic partners. "I remember thinking at the time that it made no sense, an angel investor didn't fit the model of investor we were looking for," Polese says. Then why did she cut him in for a piece? "Ron's persistence," she says. She laughs, adding that basically saying yes to Conway was much easier than saying no.

Polese's former Sun colleagues might have warned her what she was in for with Conway had she known to ask. The Personal Training Systems deal was a minor one inside Sun, but for a small company struggling to be noticed it was a prime opportunity for some free publicity. Conway lobbied hard for Sun to send out a press release announcing the deal. For weeks he was getting the runaround inside Sun, and then when finally he tracked down the right people, they always claimed to be too swamped to help him. He kept phoning until eventually one day he blew up. "I know Scott McNealy and I'm calling his ass in an hour," he threatened, invoking the name of Sun's co-founder and the company's longtime CEO. "And then a whole bunch of people are going to get fired."

The truth was Conway really didn't know McNealy. But in this case only one degree separated him and the big boss at Sun. Conway's wife, Gayle, and Susan McNealy occasionally played tennis together, so he had the McNealys' home phone number. "I was more than willing to use it," Conway says. "I had been in several meetings with him and seen him at parties, blah blah blah. Are we fast friends? Absolutely not. But he knew exactly who I was and he wouldn't have hung up on me. He'd have listened long enough to get pissed." Whom McNealy might have gotten pissed at, Conway or his underlings, isn't clear, but it's also a moot point. Conway got his press release.

—

One afternoon Conway received a frantic phone call from Hans Severiens, co-founder of the Band of Angels. Ben Rosen, the legendary venture capitalist and longtime chairman of Compaq Computer (he has since stepped down from the post), was visiting from New York and would be a special guest at that night's monthly meeting. But the two entrepreneurs who had been scheduled to pitch the group had both canceled at the last minute, and now they had no program. As Conway tells it, Severiens "thinks Ben is God," and apparently he's not the only one. At the end of that night's meeting, which took place in 1996, men well into their fifties lined up for Rosen's autograph and generally hovered around him in the fashion of ten-year-olds meeting a favorite sports star. As it turns out, Conway not only rode to Severiens's rescue, providing that night's guest entrepreneur, but he renewed a long-dormant friendship with Rosen that would eventually lead to the creation of his Angel Investors.

Conway and Rosen's relationship dates back to Conway's Altos days, when Rosen monitored the PC maker as a Morgan Stanley analyst. Rosen would attain the status of industry luminary after providing the venture funding to the three Texas Instrument employees who created Compaq at a Houston-area House of Pies, and he and Conway fell out of touch, but at that night's Band of Angels meeting Rosen saw in Conway a means to plug into the Internet frenzy sweeping through the Valley. "My connections were to an earlier generation of entrepreneurs," Rosen says. "Ron had all these connections to a whole new set of entrepreneurs." It was an odd pairing—one of the industry's éminences grises and the aggressive, sometimes overbearing salesman—but one of convenience. "Ben says to me, 'Hey, I really want to be active out here even though I'm on the East Coast. When you're looking to invest in a deal, will you show it to me?' " Conway recalls.

Despite Rosen's stature, Conway hesitated before saying yes. "Jeez, that could really slow me down," Conway told him, but Rosen promised never to let more than twenty-four hours pass without saying yes or no to a deal. Though he lived three thousand miles away, Rosen co-invested with Conway in a long list of companies. "As a venture capitalist, all you do is due diligence," Rosen says. "I was tired of the fiduciary responsibility. As an angel investor, I wanted someone else to take on that responsibility." Says Conway, "He would invest totally on my word."

Rosen would occasionally return the favor, like the time he gave Conway the heads-up on a small startup called Ask Jeeves. Upon Rosen's suggestion, Conway visited the Berkeley-based company and then phoned Rosen. "Ben, we've hit the jackpot," Conway excitedly told Rosen, and not forty-eight hours later Rosen was on his private jet heading west. The two had missed the seed round, but both were early investors in this startup whose stock would quadruple on its first day as a publicly traded company.

Rosen wasn't the only one who wanted to co-invest with Conway, and quickly word spread inside the burgeoning community of young Internet entrepreneurs that Conway was someone worth meeting. The new entrepreneurs were by and large an impatient lot, and here was Conway, in as much of a hurry as they were. Conway had a net worth in the tens of millions. He would commit to an enterprise on the spot if he liked you and your idea, and he offered a pipeline to other well-off individuals eager for the vicarious thrills of seeing their younger selves succeed. To those who wanted to piggyback with him, it didn't seem to matter that Conway never surfed the Internet: he had a good eye for talent, and maybe more important, he was eager to become a player in an environment that compensated anyone willing to take a risk. He was a dream come true, not only to those land-rush entrepreneurs who felt they didn't have a moment to waste but also to the gray hairs who already owned their big houses, their yachts, and their Tahoe chalets. The world around them had gone Internet crazy and Conway was managing to place himself at the center of it all. He offered them something more valuable than anything their riches could otherwise buy, a chance to remain vital and active.

Conway loved playing the role of facilitator. But juggling a new syndicate for each deal was proving an enormous headache, so in 1997 he created a fund he called Adam Ventures. Twenty people threw $200,000 each into Adam, and Conway invested the $4 million as he saw fit, typically in $200,000 increments.

In short order, though, $4 million didn't seem nearly enough. Every day he was meeting another set of promising founders armed with studies laying out another as-yet-untapped multibillion-dollar market. If he had more money at his disposal, he could fund all the good deals he was seeing, rather than some of them. And with a larger pool, he could also follow up on his best bets, investing side by side with the VCs in later rounds.

Conway began raising money for Angel Investors, L.P., in December 1998, delving into his Rolodex of friends and industry contacts. In two months, he had gotten commitments for $30 million, but soon $30 million proved inadequate. The ten or twenty business plans Conway was seeing each week grew to one hundred or more per week. There were also the pressures placed on the fund by everyone's raised expectations. Where only a year earlier the typical entrepreneur working on seed financing was looking for a few hundred thousand, now they were more likely to ask for $1 million, if not more.

Conway might have been frightened off by the steep price of buying even a small slice of a startup, but the entire financial ecosystem was changing accordingly. The two-person startup he bought into at the grossly inflated post-money valuation of $6 million would—if all went well—be worth $20 million in the B round six months later and $80 million in the C round the following year. No one seemed to much mind because in short order the stock market would make sure everyone was well taken care of. The traditional guidelines dic-

rating that a company demonstrate at least four straight quarters of increasing profitability, like so many of the old economic rules, no longer seemed to apply. The new mantra on Wall Street held that a company needed to sign up new customers as fast as possible and worry later about things like revenues and profits. What was the risk in paying too much for a company on the front end when the public markets were quick to offer so generous a payoff on the back end?

In November of 1998, a company called Theglobe.com went public. To some in the Valley, Theglobe's public offering represented a critical inflection point: on Friday, November 13, 1998, an overly forgiving stock market seemed to drop all pretensions of rationality. Started by two Cornell students, Theglobe sought to create an online community any way it could—through chat rooms, repackaged news feeds, stock quotes, and an advice column on love. It seemed the ultimate "concept stock"—a newly minted Wall Street term for a company that was nothing more than a concept in search of a viable business model—yet by that point the public had become completely swept up in dot-com fervor. Theglobe's stock price rose from $9 to $97 a share on its first day of trading. Suddenly this company arguably worth nothing was valued at almost $1 billion. "Theglobe.com had helped sever the relationship between profits and share price—inspiring a wave of money-losing startups to rush to market with IPOs," two reporters for *The Wall Street Journal* would write in May 2001.

Every week seemed to bring more confirmation that there was no easier way to make fast money than by getting in near the ground floor of an Internet company. Through the first six months of 1999, 218 companies went public, including Marimba and Ask Jeeves. Neither company had shown a single profitable quarter, let alone four in a row, but Marimba debuted that spring at $66 a share, giving the company a market cap of $1.6 billion, and Jeeves, which opened at $72 a share and hit a high of $174 that November, could boast of a $6 billion market cap at its peak. Conway declines to disclose the price he paid for either of these stocks, but suffice it to say, as Polese did, "that Ron has done very well on his Marimba investment." Other early investments were proving similarly lucrative, such as Dimension X, which Microsoft bought for an undisclosed price, and AtWeb, which Netscape purchased for $212 million one year after the company was created. Never in anyone's memory had making money seemed so easy.

So in the fall of 1999, Conway shook the money tree once again to raise Angel-II. This time he cast a far wider net, raising five times more than he did with Angel-I, $150 million. And why not? Another 148 companies—two per business day—went public in the last three months of the year, according to Thomson Financial. From the perspective of late 1999, the only mistake would be to have taken too modest a bite.

Chapter 3

—

IN RON WE TRUST

Conway first wrote out a list of every big Internet company he could name. This was late in the summer of 1999, so his list included Amazon.com, America Online, Cisco Systems, Yahoo, and eBay. Iomega and Infoseek made the list, as did VeriSign, CNET, Scient, and Excite@Home. He wrote down the names of the software titans working around the clock to reinvent themselves as Internet titans, such as Microsoft and Oracle, and he listed out the big investment banks successfully cashing in on the Internet boom. He was particularly keen on companies such as Hotmail, Flycast, and When.com, startups that had not been around long before being swallowed whole by a larger company anxious to stay ahead of the Internet curve. Conway figured the founders of these firms were the people with their ears closest to the ground. With Angel-II he sought to "maximize the deal flow"—to create a world in which he learned about every hot new startup earlier than any other funder.

Next Conway tried making contact with the founders and top executives at every company on his list. Some he already knew but most he didn't, so he set about figuring out who did, playing his own personal version of Six Degrees of Separation: How many calls would it take to reach someone in tight with eBay founder Pierre Omidyar? Conway was willing to cold call anyone, but the master salesman knew you don't pitch the likes of Omidyar without first getting a platinum-plated introduction.

Silicon Valley is a dauntingly massive scene, unless you're part of the in-crowd, in which case it's small and clubby if not at times claustrophobic. If sometimes it seems as if everyone in the upper echelons knows one another, that's because they typically do. The ruling tribe, even fierce competitors, tend to attend the same parties and eat at the same restaurants and invest in the same dot-coms. There are overlapping Mafias and competing Mafias, and Mafias for people of different ages and backgrounds. The younger chiefs can be found at the same San Francisco clubs after hours and they run into one another snowboarding at Heavenly, while the older hands tend to belong to the same golf and tennis clubs and send their kids to the same few exclusive nursery schools. Only once you climb to the upper echelons of the Valley's hierarchy do you discover how many deal points are worked out on the sidelines of a soccer field.

In the coming weeks, Conway's problem wouldn't be finding potential funders but drawing lines without angering those not permitted to participate. The likes of Tiger Woods and Henry Kissinger were allowed into Angel-II but not the dentist down the street who phoned about investing. "Fund one was more folksy," Conway says, but this time only those with strong Internet credentials or a famous name would be allowed in. We need you to refer promising young companies to the fund, Conway told each investor. Investors in Angel-II were also expected to occasionally work the phone or call in a chit if necessary. As Conway told them, we expect you to do what you can inside your own company and within your various networks to help an Angel startup looking for a favor. And if everyone pulls his or her own weight, together everyone grows ever richer.

"This was at the height of the Internet frenzy," Conway explains.

"Raining money was the easy part. What we wanted were connections, we wanted deal flow. We told people, 'It's not good enough just to give us your money.' "

—

Silicon Valley has its elite, but the difference between its elite and elites everywhere else is that the Valley's upper echelons are so porous. In the mid-1990s you could arrive a nobody and end up a somebody who would be embraced by the in-crowd, provided that either you were an integral member of a company that had invented something breathtakingly new or you had grown monumentally wealthy in short order. Accomplishing both those feats, of course, meant that the embrace was likely to be that much warmer and deeper. An MBA from Stanford or Harvard helped, but it might even have been irrelevant once your net worth crossed into the eight digits—as Conway's own career has proven. "It's a very open elite," says the Institute for the Future's Paul Saffo, a forecaster who every year hosts a dinner in Davos, Switzerland, for A-list nerds attending the World Economic Forum. "Anyone can get in."

Let's say you had sold your fourteen-month-old company to Yahoo for $200 million in 1999. Once the press release hit the wires, it was as if a red velvet rope had been lifted. You were ushered into quarters you never knew existed, like the wood-paneled, rich red leather world of the Private Wealth Management offices inside every investment bank in the Bay Area. There your personal banker would periodically invite you to flip a hot IPO, so the 1,000 shares of InstantRiches.com you bought in the morning for $12,000 were worth $54,000 by the time your new best friend sold them later in the day. Suddenly you felt like Hillary Clinton, invited to turn a $1,000 bet on cattle futures into a quick $100,000.

The invitations poured in. One of the Valley's king-of-the-hill VCs, the same guy who never quite got around to funding you (he never quite said no, either, because the good ones never do), invited you to invest in a "side fund," a multimillion-dollar semisecret pot of money that piggybacked on the firm's hottest deals. By that point you had heard from any number of people that if *ever* you get a chance to invest in one of these things it's *mandatory* because the returns are a guaranteed ten-bagger, an investment that will return to you ten times your original outlay. You were asked to serve on the boards of directors or boards of advisers of a few of the Valley's choicest companies (in either case options were part of the deal), the right people offered to help your children get into the right private schools. In short order life felt like you'd been permanently bumped from coach to first class and, like the steamed hand towels and glass goblets offered by the flight attendants when you sit in the fore of the cabin, the perks and indulgences came to be expected. That's about when you heard from Conway, who helped welcome you into the club by inviting you into a fund that seemed to include anybody who was anybody. The minimum entry fee, $50,000, was low, for this crowd at least, so you signed up to participate in the magic alchemy that was Ron Conway if for no other reason than you wanted to feel part of a club that includes the likes of Marc Andreessen, Ben Rosen, Esther Dyson, Tiger, and Shaq. Besides, the parties were supposedly great.

There's the digital divide between the races, of course, and the equally troublesome digital divide between the haves and have-nots. But there's another digital divide, the divide between the haves and the have-everythings that seems particularly wide in Silicon Valley. The haves live comfortably, and even if they don't own property given the preposterous price of real estate in the Bay Area, they have their 401(k) and occasionally vacation in Hawaii and Cabo. Yet only the have-everythings were welcomed into this giant alumni association where everyone helped one another out when they could. The have-everythings were invited into the choicest side funds and they were given a small slice of equity to sit on a hot new startup's advisory board—and they were invited to own a slice of Ron Conway. The only caveat, whether you joined a side fund, an advisory board, or Angel Investors, was that you should lend a hand when you could.

"We told people straight out, 'If you're with Yahoo, and we need a commerce deal with Yahoo, you'll at least pick up the phone and listen to us,' " Conway says.

"People part of the club tend to help each other freely," says a young entrepreneur named Jad Duwaik, who bumped up against this less-dissected digital divide shortly after arriving in the Bay Area in 1999. "If you're in the club, you can do someone a favor and trust that somehow you're going to get repaid for that favor. Favors are exchanged much more freely among the have-everythings than among the rest of us, because the rest of us, when we're doing a favor, we're looking for some kind of tangible payoff." The typical "have" might do a favor for a relative stranger but based on a careful calculation: in exchange for my time and my trouble, what's in it for me? Among the have-everythings, though, "there's no need for someone to reciprocate right away because they know that over time their favor will continue to mean something because they all remain within the club. At some point some day they know there's going to be an opportunity to reciprocate," Duwaik says.

Most have-everythings don't consider themselves have-everythings. The fatted calf conservatively worth $20 million who participates in several side funds and exudes a rested glow one sees only in the very wealthy hardly views himself as a have-everything because he lives in such close proximity to people who can drive around in $300,000 sports cars. To him the real have-everythings are Larry Ellison and John Doerr. Ellison resented the late-night curfew imposed on jet landings at San Jose International Airport, so at the start of 2000 he bankrolled a federal lawsuit against the city and landed his $38 million Gulfstream V whenever he wanted, thumbing his nose at the threats of legal action by city officials. Doerr cruises the Valley in the back of a minivan outfitted with a satellite dish so that the World's Greatest Venture Capitalist can be productive every moment of every day.

And there's this man who is godfather to so many of the Valley's have-everythings, Conway himself, with whom to contrast themselves. His Atherton home may be modest by Valley standards—"he lives in the kind of house that's being torn down somewhere in Atherton at any given moment," says one sometime guest—but there's also the penthouse apartment high atop San Francisco's Nob Hill with the

private elevator and sublime views that Conway bought fully fur-
nished at the height of the frenzy for $2.5 million for those few days
a month he has meetings in San Francisco. (Staying overnight in the
city is more convenient than commuting the forty-five minutes down
the peninsula.) A true have-everything hobnobs with the likes of
Goldie Hawn on a 151-foot yacht anchored off the French Riviera
and, like Conway, thinks little of paying $20,000 to charter a round-
trip private jet to fly a small group to Las Vegas for a weekend. Newcomers might be invited into a couple of side funds, but Conway has
been playing the side fund game for years, turning millions into tens
of millions during the richest of bull markets.

Conway didn't have to sell Angel-II very hard, at least not in Silicon Valley. Some people he sold over the phone or in a single breakfast or lunch. Others were given a phone number and code so, at their
convenience, they could call in to hear a recorded version of Conway's spiel. Still others he pitched in group meetings he hosted every
few weeks in a conference room in Redwood Shores. His main selling point was the magic of a fund that brought together so many
well-connected Internet insiders. With so much eager cash flowing
through the Valley, the collective connections of his investors would
serve as an enticing lure, no small advantage when vying for an invite from the most sought-after entrepreneurs. "It helps to be able to
tell an entrepreneur that we have a pipeline into any big Internet company they could name," Conway says.

"It's not like Ron made people sign anything, but there was a
clearly stated set of expectations," says Bob Bozeman, whom Conway would hire as a general partner to help him run Angel Investors.
"And Ron was willing to read people the riot act if they didn't meet
those expectations."

The intangibles of participating in Angel-II no doubt played a large
part in the decision of many who ended up investing. Playing angel to
the Valley's most promising startups meant a chance to remain current
about activity bubbling up on the outer edges of the entrepreneurial
universe. Many of the Valley's Younger Turks were honored to have
been tapped on the shoulder by someone of Conway's stature; others

aw wider financial benefits beyond the fund's performance. By committing a tiny fraction of their fortune, they could expand their personal network and spend time with these fidgety-smart and engaging young entrepreneurs, many of whom were no doubt going places. "You're better off being part of Ron's network than being outside his network," says venture capitalist Lise Buyer, who was a top analyst at Credit Suisse First Boston when Conway invited her into his fund.

—

So who's in Angel Investors?

The lions in winter were well represented, of course, or those Conway dubbed "the really old guys, like Ben Rosen and Bob Peters, the first vice president of marketing at Cisco." Dean Morton, the retired chief operating officer at Hewlett-Packard, is an investor, as are Jim Gibbons, former dean of engineering at Stanford University; Macromedia co-founder Bud Colligan; former 3Com CEO Bill Krause; and David Duffield, the co-founder of PeopleSoft and a man with a net worth that exceeded $3 billion in 1999. Sandy Robertson, of Robertson Stephens fame, is also an investor.

Bill Joy is an investor. If the computer world elected people annually to a Computer Hall of Fame, Joy would be a lock on a first-round ballot. As a graduate student at UC-Berkeley twenty years ago, he wrote a version of the Unix operating system that even today serves as the foundation for a large share of the Web's central servers. He's the co-founder of Sun Microsystems and someone Conway dubbed "a real good pedigree investor." Conway didn't really know Joy, but Joy called him out of the blue to ask if he could invest. "He had heard about the fund from somebody and for him it was, 'Hell, yes,' " Conway says. Conway speculates that Joy's motivation for investing was that he saw Angel Investors as a window on the Web. Certainly he didn't need the money.

Esther Dyson isn't the only person on Conway's list to have served as the subject of a long *Vanity Fair* profile, but she ranks as maybe his highest-profile technology investor. For more than fifteen years, Dyson has hosted PC Forum, one of the computer world's two must-attend conferences, and she's also the publisher of the influential industry newsletter *Release 1.0*. As the head of EDventure, she's a globe-trotting venture capitalist. She writes a weekly syndicated newspaper column, and when Conway approached her about Angel-II she was serving as interim chairperson of ICANN (the Internet Corporation for Assigned Names and Numbers), the nonprofit the federal government created to take over administration of Internet-based domain names. "Esther is busy with her own thing, but when we ask her she helps," Conway says. The connection proves particularly helpful in the months leading up to PC Forum, when a long queue of startups beg for a moment in the spotlight on Dyson's stage. "Because they're an Angel company doesn't mean they're going to get in," Conway says. "But I can get on the phone and plead the case and a lot of people can't."

Microsoft is an investor, as are Amazon and Compaq. Each company invested a couple of million each. Several former Microsoft employees are investors, including Pete Higgins, a former Microsoft vice president who headed the team that produced the original Microsoft Office suite and then led the company's earliest online consumer business efforts. Carol Bartz, the CEO of Autodesk, is a perennial of feature articles touting the top women in the industry and also an investor, as is Informix founder Roger Sippl.

Venture capitalists were not invited to invest in Angel Investors. Conway didn't want portfolio companies to feel any pressure on that front when looking to raise future financing. (Several are in the fund anyway because they took VC jobs once they had already invested.) Conway didn't adopt the same rule with the investment banks. "Investment banks take companies public, so we let them in," Conway explains. Inside the world of technology investment banking, there's a Big Three: Morgan Stanley Dean Witter, Goldman Sachs, and Credit Suisse First Boston. If that world has a single star, it's Frank Quattrone, who heads Credit Suisse's Palo Alto–based Technology Group. Quattrone is an investor, as is Brad Koenig, Quattromo's counterpart at Goldman Sachs. A group from Morgan Stanley pooled together a couple of million dollars and invested it as one, according to Conway.

The typical Angel-II investor threw in $250,000. Some invested $100,000, a small minority wrote a check for the minimum $50,000. A few individuals invested $1 million or more. By law, each investor had to swear that he or she had a net worth of at least $1 million, but more than four fifths of the 545 people who invested in either Angel-I or Angel-II were worth more than $5 million. That helps explain why at least some people threw in $100,000 even if they had no idea if Angel Investors would make them money or not. Back then, the Valley's heaviest hitters were spinning off so much in profits each year that they could use the tax write-off.

There's no official count on the number of billionaires in Angel-II, but there are at least a few. eBay founder Pierre Omidyar is an investor, as is Jeff Skoll, the man Omidyar chose as his partner when he elected to quit his day job in 1996 and get *serious* about this online swapping thing. By the time Conway contacted the two of them two thirds of the way through 1999, Omidyar was thirty-two and worth $3.7 billion and Skoll, thirty-three, worth $1.4 billion. Pehong Chan, a Taiwanese immigrant who founded (among other companies) BroadVision, was worth $1.7 billion at the end of 1999. He, too, is an investor. Conway approached Yahoo co-founders David Filo and Jerry Yang about investing (the two had a combined net worth of $6.2 billion in the fall of 1999), but both turned him down, as did Yahoo's then CEO, Tim Koogle, another billionaire. Conway lists three former Yahoo execs among his investors and also Yahoo board member Eric Hippeau (another billionaire after CNET purchased Ziff Davis, the magazine conglomerate over which he presided as CEO), but no one who currently works for the company.

"People at Yahoo conflicted out," Conway explains. That was the most common reason he would hear when people declined his invitation to invest. "When we got turndowns," he says, "it was because people thought there'd be a conflict of interest. 'Hey, I work in the M and A [mergers and acquisitions] department, there's a good chance we'll be acquiring some of these companies, I can't invest.' " Even a good friend told him no because he recognized Conway would not be shy about calling in his chits. "I knew I'd be doing hundreds of favors for Ron, so I decided against investing in Angel Investors," says this man, who holds a top post at an important Valley-based company. "I didn't want anyone accusing me of making decisions in my job for my personal financial gain." He says he has performed countless favors for Conway—but because he had no financial stake in Angel Investors, no one could accuse him of flouting any ethical guidelines.

Most inside Conway's network, however, didn't embrace that same cautious attitude. "Different people have different screens," he says. Among those Conway approached who also said no: Sun's Scott McNealy, the top team at Excite@Home, and eBay CEO Meg Whitman. Still, Conway estimates that only one in every four people he approached turned him down.

At least a few people said no for reasons beyond the potential for conflicts of interest. One long-standing member of the Silicon Valley elite is in his share of side funds, but he drew the line at Conway. "It's not sinister what Ron is trying to do," he says. "He's only systematized what people have been doing in the Valley for a long time. You've got all these people who know each other real well and they're used to helping each other out and profiting from each other." The bottom line, though, was that he did not want to feel beholden to this man he refers to as "Ron the con."

"Ron is a charming guy," he says, "but he's always got an angle."

"When someone said no we were disappointed but moved on," Conway says. "Once I got two or three investors out of eBay, I didn't care as much if a Meg Whitman said no. It was move on and make sure I had Excite covered." Eric Greenberg, the founder of the Web consulting company Scient, and Halsey Minor, founder of CNET, were both worth $355 million in mid-1999; both are Angel investors. So is Sky Dayton, the founder of EarthLink, the world's third most popular online service.

The Internet's overexposed poster boy, Marc Andreessen, twenty-four years old when he appeared on the cover of *Newsweek* barefoot and sitting on a golden throne, is an investor. So is Kim Polese, the Marimba co-founder who in 1997 was dubbed by one trade magazine "the hottest Web celebrity since Netscape poster boy Marc Andreessen." People could have said the same about another Angel investor, Indian-born Sabeer Bhatia, who sold the company he co-founded, Hotmail, to Microsoft for $400 million that same year. "In Silicon Valley, that deal made Bhatia a brand name," *The Industry Standard*'s Jonathan Rabinovitz wrote. "In India, it turned him into a superstar as big as Michael Jordan is in the United States."

If one company more than any other jump-started the Valley's Internet boom, it was Netscape, which AOL bought for $4.2 billion in 1998. Naturally there's a huge contingent of Netscape alums inside Angel Investors. "Dozens of our investors" trace their roots back to Netscape, says Jane Rush, a Netscape veteran who helped Conway handle the paperwork nightmare required to put together Angel-II, which alone had more than four hundred investors.

Conway was at his most aggressive when pursuing the founders of recently acquired companies, people such as Bhatia, and Tony Hsieh and Alfred Lin, two twentysomethings who sold their two-year-old company, LinkExchange, to Microsoft for $265 million in 1998. Ram Shriram is a former Netscape executive who in 1997 started Junglee, a company he sold to Amazon for $190 million in Amazon stock less than two years later. Shriram stood to make countless millions more in stock options had he stayed as a top boss at Amazon, but he quit not long after arriving in Seattle, a prescient move only in retrospect. At the time, he seemed to be walking away from a veritable fortune. Inside the Valley's formidable Indian community, Shriram is viewed as a star, an A-list player who has invested his own money in roughly two dozen startups. Shriram is also an investor in both Angel-I and Angel-II, though he describes his investments as "nothing significant." Conway and Shriram met while Shriram was still at Netscape and Conway was trying to cut a deal whereby Netscape sold a CD-ROM prepared by Conway's computer training company to its corporate customers. "He wouldn't take no for an answer and I like that," Shriram says.

Joe Beninato is a co-founder of When.com, an online calendar company that AOL bought for roughly $200 million less than one year after it was formed. After the sale, Beninato was deluged by offers, from cold-calling Merrill Lynch brokers to overly familiar real estate agents to acquaintances wanting him to play angel to their startup dreams. He considered a long list of options, including side funds and several angel-style investments, but Conway's invitation was one of the few he accepted. He had heard of Conway but knew little about the man, so he started phoning around.

"People said that he's probably the most well-connected guy in the Valley. And if he wasn't the most well connected, then in the top few," Beninato says. "He has connections on Sand Hill Road. He's got connections to industry old-timers and to the new stars like Andreessen." Not everyone was sure Conway had the best track record for picking winners, but none doubted that if a hot deal came along, Conway would get a look. So Beninato invested, as did his three When.com co-founders, and also the founders from AtWeb, Flycast, NooHoo, and a long list of other startups sold to larger companies at steep premiums.

"In a business setting you can say I'm very competitive," Conway says. "If I decide I want something to happen, I try *real* hard to make it happen." And reaching the business world's newest Masters of the Universe, these well-connected first-generation Internet stars, was a goal that had Conway "very, very motivated."

—

Conway took his first of four trips to Los Angeles to troll for investors in September 1999. He checked himself into The Peninsula Beverly Hills, a posh four-star hotel where rooms range between $325 and $3,000 per night, and for two days he sold his fund in back-to-back meetings. No one had heard of Conway in LA, but they wanted to believe. He boasted about all his big-name Internet investors and their corporate connections. He explained how he would have first crack at the hottest deals, and he ticked off the six companies in which he invested that by that time had gone public, including Marimba and Jeeves. He spoke, too, about the companies that had been sold for a fast profit: the several hundred million dollars AOL had paid for Spinner.com; Dimension X, bought by Microsoft for an undisclosed price; and BuyDirect.com, which Beyond.com bought for $134 million. He didn't have to sell himself very hard, Conway says, not at the height of the madness. "People in southern California were more excited about the Internet than even in northern California," Conway says.

Tony Perkins, publisher of the *Red Herring,* made two key introductions that helped Conway make connections inside LA's entertainment world. The *Herring* is a trade publication focused on the world of venture capital, yet apparently Perkins thought nothing of doing favors for this man regularly quoted inside its pages. (Perkins declined comment, perhaps because I work for *The Industry Standard,* a *Herring* rival.) Conway knew the first man he needed to meet in LA was Jeff Berg, but the question was how? Perkins took care of the introductions between Berg and Conway, and he also introduced Conway to the financier Herb Allen. Allen, famous for the annual confab he hosts for billion-dollar deal makers in his Sun Valley, Idaho, hunting lodge, is also an Angel-II investor.

Berg is the chairman, CEO, and part owner of International Creative Management (ICM), one of Hollywood's top talent agencies. (Barbra Streisand, Mel Gibson, and Arnold Schwarzenegger are among ICM's clients.) Berg sits on the board of directors of the software giant Oracle, and at the time he also served on Excite's board, which places him squarely at the intersection of Hollywood and the Internet. Apparently Berg and Conway got along famously. "He was my springboard," Conway says. "Mainly every media person I met in Los Angeles came through Jeff." Conway's connections to Intel also helped (three of its executives or former executives are investors). Intel has widespread connections in southern California because its chips must anticipate whatever multimedia marvels the entertainment industry might have in development.

Through his Intel connections Conway met Leonard Armato, an agent turned Internet entrepreneur even as he handled the business affairs of the likes of Shaq, Kareem Abdul-Jabbar, boxer Oscar De La Hoya, and Pamela Anderson. Armato had spotted the money-making potential of the Internet long before most. In 1996, Armato moved the website Shaq.com from Microsoft's MSN to SportsLine.com, breaking new ground by negotiating an equity stake in CBS SportsLine USA on O'Neal's behalf. By the time Conway stepped into Armato's office to talk about Angel Investors, Armato and Shaq were busy building Dunk.net, a site that would sell sneakers and other athletic gear bearing the Dunk.net name, and also a second site called AliveSports.com with De La Hoya. Like Berg, Armato would prove one of Conway's key southern California contacts.

Conway didn't meet directly with the truly famous. Shaq ended up an investor because of Armato. Schwarzenegger also got in through his agent, who was an investor as well. Henry Kissinger had created an investment fund with a business partner who knew Ben Rosen, and for Conway that was enough: both were granted a seat at the table. Kay Koplowitz, the former head of the USA Network, is an investor, as is Randy Cross, a former football player who is now a sports commentator, and James Robinson III, the former chairman of American Express. "We basically told these people, 'If you really want to get in the fund and you can review the docs expeditiously and take no exceptions, we're happy to have you . . . but we're not going to spend a lot of time on you,' " Conway says.

At first Conway figured he might raise $75 million for Angel-II, but demand swelled as word spread. Conway kept extending the deadline for closing the fund, from October to November until finally, as 1999 was coming to a close, he was approaching the legal limit for keeping it open. In the end he raised $150 million. The logistics on a fund with hundreds of individual investors would prove to be an administrative nightmare, but to Conway all the headaches and delays were worth it. He created what he described as a "giant club" in which "you didn't want to let down other members of the club. So people really did whatever they could to help our companies. There was this real pressure for everyone to perform."

Chapter 4

—

MONEY, MONEY EVERYWHERE

John Conway was already feeling more than a little sour about the new world driving past his Chevron station on El Camino Real in the heart of Silicon Valley. For more than twenty-five years, Ron Conway's oldest brother has owned a filling station in the self-satisfied town of Menlo Park, sandwiched between Atherton to the north and Palo Alto to the south and home to most of the area's best-known venture capital firms. Everyone always in such a hurry. No one ever taking the time to say hello. John Conway recalls a much quainter, quieter time, when he knew his regulars' names and they knew his. Lots of important business transpired in the PC age, yet even then most people seemed to take time for the basics, like a smile and a "Hello, how are you?"

"Now it's all this fast-lane attitude," he grouses. Everyone goggle-eyed with stress, everyone impatient, people yapping into their cell phones about next rounds and b-to-b's and Lord knows what else.

And then one day the word got out that his brother was Ron Conway.

The two brothers, born three years apart, are the spitting image of each other. They have the same aquiline Conway nose, the same deep blue eyes, the same ruddy complexion, the same thin lips, and the same set to the chin. Like his younger brother, John Conway, too, has prematurely white hair and wears steel-framed glasses. Gather a hundred people into a room and it might take you a minute and a half to figure out that these two are brothers.

There is no shortage of tableaus that captured the frenzy of Silicon Valley at the tail end of the Internet boom, but one strong candidate would be a scene that repeated itself on the oil-stained tarmac of the Menlo Chevron in 1999, sometimes as often as two or three times a week. Picture drivers in their twenties, in a perky new Volkswagen Jetta or shiny BMW. Add a pair of sunglasses and the slicked-back hair for those who arrived with a Stanford MBA in their back pocket. Half the time they let their engines run and music blare as they said, "I need to talk to Ron Conway." (You'd think they'd say hello. You'd think they'd at least introduce themselves. A little common decency.) They'd blather the same noise they jabbered into their cell phones, talking about their end-to-end e-solutions for the enterprise, or their back-end best-of-breed infrastructure plays. John Conway was part of his brother's world but he wasn't; he was a regular at his famous brother's parties, but he'd stand off to the side with hands in pockets, staring wide-eyed at the monied class milling about the yard. These young people would arrive at his gas station, but he could comprehend only their intensity.

"I'd try to get in touch with Ron for them," he says. "It seemed so important to them." But then he'd phone his brother (leaving a message, of course—he was never available by phone back then) and Ron would be exasperated. Tell them I'm too busy, he'd instruct his older brother. Have them send me an e-mail—which he'd then delete because he entertained proposals only from people endorsed by someone part of his network. All that education and for what? Did they really think he would meet every Tom, Dick, and Jane who hassled his brother for an introduction?

—

Angel Investors wasn't a few months old before Conway realized he needed help. He was getting deluged with business plans. The over-the-transom proposals were dealt with swiftly, with a polite one-paragraph thanks-but-no-thanks note. The pitches that came through an investor, or at least dropped the name of a pedigreed member of the club, were something else entirely. Each had to be read through and responded to thoughtfully, which is why he hired Bob Bozeman as a partner in January of 1999.

Bozeman was available and Bozeman was also a good complement in a yin-yang way. Bozeman was also an accident. One of the first companies in which Conway invested after founding Angel Investors, CarStation.com, was looking for a top executive to help them realize their dream of creating an online community for automotive repair professionals. (Go figure.) Conway immediately thought of Bozeman, who, after leaving Altos, had moved to southern California to run a Santa Barbara–based business that sold computerized diagnostic tools to mechanics. The two had kept in touch in the intervening years. Occasionally, Conway would phone his old colleague to invite him to throw maybe fifty grand into some company he had discovered, but Bozeman, who had arrived at Altos after the company had gone public, didn't have that kind of money. At the start of 1999, though, Conway phoned Bozeman to invite him to share in the bonanza without having to put up a dime. Did he want a top spot inside CarStation?

Bozeman jumped at the offer, but then the day before he was supposed to start at CarStation, Conway broached the partnership idea. Bozeman had a tech background, so he could assess the technical viability of a proposal. But mainly what Conway says he saw in his old colleague was someone whom he wouldn't have to waste much time breaking in. "He knew my modus operandi," Conway says. "I knew he could just come and start working and know how I worked."

The only hang-up, aside from some disappointed people at

CarStation, was Bozeman's moderate-sized brokerage account. Those in the business call it "skin in the game"—the cash many professional money managers sink into their own fund to demonstrate to investors that they are confident they'll show a handsome return. Conway suggested that Bozeman throw in a promissory note for $500,000. Once the fund started generating a profit, he'd pay the loan back. Of course it'd be a major-league headache for everyone involved if the fund never made a profit, but that seemed a preposterous thought in 1999. There's no way the fund could actually *lose* money, was there?

—

Bozeman is a jovial man in his early fifties with a sweet disposition and an easy smile. He's short, about five feet four inches tall, with a bowling-ball build, neatly trimmed brown hair that is always perfectly in place, and blue eyes that twinkle behind a set of oversize round glasses. He is diligent and eager to please, and exhibits a *serious* Type A personality that requires him to read and, if appropriate, respond to every last e-mail in his inbox before retiring to bed each night, and then set his alarm so he has an hour to blast through whatever mail has accumulated overnight.

Eager to prove to his old colleague that he had chosen well, Bozeman immediately threw himself into the job. He and his wife of thirty-two years rented a modest-sized town house in Foster City, a bedroom community a fifteen-minute drive from Conway's home. He knew nothing about angel investing before moving back to the Bay Area, so his learning curve was steep. The work pace would have been brutal even if he were a seasoned pro, so he put off looking for a home to buy. Only after it was too late did Bozeman calculate that, given the steep rise in the average price of a home in Silicon Valley, his procrastination probably cost him a few hundred thousand dollars.

"Have I mentioned to you that I haven't had a personal life in the past two years?" Bozeman asked me early in 2001. (Actually he had, in a previous interview.) He and his wife flew to Paris in the fall of 2000, but that was about it for breaks except the rare day off. He describes his life, and also Conway's, as a "nonstop treadmill. There was never a moment of private life. In either of our lives."

Prior to Bozeman's arrival, Conway had no system for investing his money. "Basically if Ron liked you," said the founder of one Angel Investors portfolio company, "he funded you." Apparently Conway *really* liked Artie Wu, a sharp young entrepreneur who had only recently earned his Stanford MBA when the two met for coffee in Mountain View late in 1998. Wu was there at the suggestion of Kleiner Perkins's Russ Siegelman, who says of Conway, "In those days he was writing six-hundred-thousand-dollar checks for anything that moved, as far as I could tell." Over coffee, Wu told Conway about a company he was then calling Facilitas. Less than sixty minutes later, Conway was ready to cut a check, but Wu hesitated. He had the names of several other angels and thought it would be rash to make any commitments before he had a chance to meet with anyone else.

By their next meeting, though, with Christmas fast approaching, Wu wished he had jumped at Conway's initial offer. The other angels were already off on holiday, and he had no money. "At that point," Wu says, "Ron really could have squeezed me. 'Hey, here's my term sheet, take it or leave it.' But instead he asks me, 'Do you need any money to tide you through the next few weeks?' " Wu asked for $50,000, and Conway told him that'd be no problem; he'd have a check written by day's end. If we do a deal, Conway said, explaining his terms, this will represent the first $50,000 I invest in your company. If you end up choosing someone other than Angel Investors, return the money plus 8 percent interest. Conway asked Wu to spell out the deal in a promissory note. "He didn't even have me write the note right then," Wu says. Later that day, with the check already deposited in a bank, he faxed Conway a term sheet.

"Ron didn't do a lot of what your average venture capitalist would see as due diligence," says Jennifer Bailey, a former Netscape executive and an Angel Investor. "He's not nitpicking through the financials or in your shorts looking at the technology. . . . Mainly he trusts his gut based on meeting someone face-to-face."

Bozeman might have known little about the world of venture funding, but he immediately devised a more rigorous system for sorting through the hundred-plus business pitches Conway and Bozeman figured they received each week in 1999. Angel Investors hired an industry veteran named Paul White to help them choose the fifteen or so sets of entrepreneurs they'd invite to pitch their plans in person. Bozeman described each company in an e-mail that he sent around to the Angel investors list once or twice a week. In theory, the notice served as a perfect guard against investing in a business category already occupied by a serious player, and occasionally they'd hear back from someone, "I hear this space is hot," or "Hey, there's already a gorilla in this space." But in reality those on the receiving end were often so busy that many of them hit delete rather than wade through Bozeman's list.

Tryouts were held every Tuesday and Thursday in the same conference room Conway used to pitch potential investors in his fund. Conway only sometimes came to these sessions, usually opting to meet one-on-one with those entrepreneurs whose deals were so hot they could circumvent the hassles of a formal pitch. Bozeman, White, and the occasional guest investor would sit around a huge blond conference table in Redwood City listening to entrepreneurs whose pitches ranged from the inspiring to the horrible. Bozeman tried capping the pitches at eight a day, but Conway or someone else part of Angel Investors would invariably slip in another startup or two. There were plenty of sessions that went from seven in the morning to seven at night, during which time they listened to back-to-back pitches and the outside world was only something they stared out at through a window.

Inside Angel Investors, they prided themselves on the instant feedback they gave entrepreneurs invited to meet them face-to-face. Those who had delivered lousy presentations and therefore stood no chance of receiving any money were told right then and there where they had gone wrong and given pointers so that they might have better luck the next time they met with a potential funder. As Bozeman explains it, they had two motivations for this. One was the Angel Investors prime directive that first and foremost they were about helping entrepreneurs. The other was that it couldn't hurt their reputations if word spread that they were such great guys that they dispensed free advice even after they decided they weren't interested in funding you. "In a market that was as hot as it was during the frenzy, every leg up helped," Bozeman says.

Maybe one in every ten companies that came to one of the regular Tuesday or Thursday meetings ended up receiving funding from Angel Investors. Companies didn't have to wait long to learn their fate. "The rule was that we would take no more than ten days to turn around a deal," Bozeman says. But even ten days was an eternity inside Angel Investors. They typically spent a day or two on due diligence before making up their minds. "That's pure Ron," Bozeman continues. "Ron is a do-it-now type of guy, and he burns a do-it-now mentality into everyone around him. You needed that attitude in those days. If you didn't move fast, you lost the hot deals." The typical Angel-I investment ranged between $100,000 and $250,000. Yet the average commitment under Angel-II was $500,000 or more.

———

Bozeman habitually carries around two cell phones. In his right pocket is a black one, in his left a slim blue one that he calls "the Ron phone." The first time we met was for lunch at an Il Fornaio in Burlingame. When the phone in his right pocket rang, he excused himself and politely switched it to mute for our meal. The Ron phone rang four times, a summons he promptly answered each time before it could ring twice. Bozeman and Conway are both general partners, but in reality Bozeman is more like the chief of staff to Conway the president. As Bozeman describes it, the two of them have an "inside-outside" relationship. Conway represents the fund to the wider world while Bozeman makes sure the trains run on time.

Both are white men hovering around the age of fifty who've been involved in the computer industry since the 1970s, but in ways crucial to Angel Investors they are polar opposites. Bozeman ran a product development department of several thousand people at Wang Laboratories back when Wang was a word processing giant; in contrast, Conway would be hard-pressed to load a new program on his computer if his son Danny wasn't home. Conway could get himself into a jam by saying too much, while Bozeman's problem is usually that he doesn't say nearly enough. Bozeman is methodical and cautious, precise and efficient, a highly organized nuts-and-bolts type who, borrowing from the tradition of IBM's Tom Watson, taped the word "THINK!" above his PC. By temperament, Bozeman is a value investor who considers Warren Buffett, famously tech-phobic, his investment hero, and he believes strongly in creating systems rich with checks and balances. Conway—well, Conway is Conway. "Ron is a speculator," Bozeman says. "He has this great nose. He trusts his gut. My role is to serve as the inspector."

At first Conway faithfully attended Bozeman's twice-a-week pitch meetings. But as the weeks passed his attendance slacked off until eventually he showed up only for those presentations he specifically wanted to see. In part that was because he was busy raising the $150 million for Angel-II, but mainly Conway couldn't let go of his own unique style of investing. What if he learned that the founders of a company touted as the next eBay were looking for investors? Was he going to tell them to wait until next Thursday, when there might be an opening on Bozeman's pitch calendar? The truth was that if you could secure an hour with Conway one-on-one and Conway was impressed with you and your idea, you'd get your money without the hassles of a formal pitch. It drove Bozeman crazy in a good-natured, I-love-this-guy-and-his-nose kind of way.

Sometimes Bozeman would join Conway on these side expeditions, especially if Conway believed he needed someone with technical expertise. In August 1999, Conway heard about a company called Octopus. Octopus typified the new, better-endowed

Silicon Valley startup, in which the company's core product was banged out not in a garage but in the wood-paneled study of a Palo Alto home at an antique Louis XIV desk. The two founders had struck gold once before with a software company the pair eventually sold for enough money to set up each for life. By the time they approached Conway, they had a working prototype for their website management tool and had recently added a third person to their team, Steve Douty, who had been a top executive at Hotmail and then a project director at Microsoft after the software giant purchased the free e-mail service. In an environment in which even the most inexperienced management team or sketchiest of business ideas could secure funding, those behind Octopus had both the experience and at least a rough-cut version of its product. They weren't the kind of team you'd pencil in on a regular Tuesday or Thursday, so Conway and Bozeman showed up at the house of one of the founders for a ninety-minute demo. Conway didn't even stay for the entire pitch. He met the trio in the flesh, judged them to be a winning team, and unless Bozeman told him otherwise he knew Angel Investors would be good for a few hundred thousand dollars.

"Back then you could get funding for practically anything," Douty says. "But we didn't just want to get checks from our relatives. We wanted to get a credible source of initial funding."

More often than not, though, Conway flew solo. "I was the Lone Ranger, so to speak," Conway says. "I was trying to get into the really high-pedigree deals that weren't necessarily looking to go through an angel round. Those are the deals that investors love." Those were also the most expensive deals to buy into, but Conway was convinced they'd prove worth it no matter what the price. "If you're going to build a company like a Yahoo, Ask Jeeves, or eBay, you should not be worried about valuation on the front end," Conway told the *Red Herring* in 1999. "If you're worried, then you must not have confidence that you're going to build a large, significant company. . . . The bottom line is if the idea is great, you're going to end up with a multibillion [-dollar] market cap and everyone is going to make more money than they can ever spend."

Conway spent much of 1999 driving the freeways and surface streets of Silicon Valley, eating lunches up and down the peninsula. And when he wasn't eating lunch he was sipping coffee at Le Boulanger in Mountain View or Chardonnay at Chantilly's later in the day. Conway and Bozeman both worked out of their homes, so their offices moved depending on the person they were meeting. People driving south from San Francisco would meet at Bacchanal in South San Francisco or Il Fornaio in Burlingame, where Conway once held so many back-to-back meetings the $100 tip he left was more a rent payment than a gratuity. He met anyone living mid-peninsula or south at a place five or ten minutes from his home, at Carpaccio's or Café Barrone in Menlo Park, or Buck's in Woodside, the favored meeting place among the VC set. And there was always Perry's in Palo Alto, a restaurant in which Conway was the second-largest shareholder against his better judgment.

When.com co-founder Joe Beninato was a regular on Conway's circuit. Beninato was everything Conway was looking for from junior members of the network. He was smart, plugged-in, and ambitious, thirty-two years old in 1999 yet already a veteran of several successful startups. Though this engineer turned marketer had scored big as one of the four co-founders of When.com and could afford to take as long a hiatus as he desired, he chose to remain busy, working as a consultant to a half-dozen startups and dabbling as an angel investor.

Beninato recalled a breakfast with Conway in the spring of 1999, at the Il Fornaio in Palo Alto. Conway arrived late carting a thick stack of papers held in color-coded files. Every five minutes someone would interrupt their conversation to pat Conway on the back and say hello. He and Beninato made some small talk before Conway peppered him with questions: What are you up to nowadays? What's hot? What are you hearing? On that occasion Beninato told Conway about a company going by a code name, the Springfield Project. That piqued Conway's interest—a company so hot its founders felt it necessary to operate under a stealth name. (Springfield is the fictional town that Homer and Marge Simpson call home.) He had never heard of the Springfield Project, but, as Beninato describes it, he was intrigued. "He was like, 'What's that? I want to put money in that. How do I get in?'" Beninato remembers. Though Beninato offered the sketchiest of descriptions—he told Conway only that the company was created to cash in on the small-business market—Conway was all over him to set him up with the company's co-founder and CEO, Andrew Beebe. "I can give Andrew a call and see if he's interested," Beninato said.

"Give me his number," Conway said. "I'll call him today." That was Conway, "generally less concerned," Beninato says, "with what a company does than whether it's hot."

Several months earlier, when seeking a first round of funding, Beebe had tried to reach Conway, with no luck. He was about to close on a sizable second round with two of the venture world's better-regarded firms, Mayfield Ventures and U.S. Venture Partners, when Conway phoned. Angel Investors had already invested in one of the Springfield Project's rivals, SmartAge.com, but that didn't seem to bother him. "He was all over us," Beebe says.

Beebe was polite but firm: poised to close on a new round of financing, they weren't seeking additional investors. Beebe may have known who Conway was, but at that point he still didn't know with whom he was dealing. One prominent trade magazine had named the Springfield Project one of ten companies to watch in 1999, and Beebe had recently been invited to present at Esther Dyson's PC Forum. The more Conway learned about the company, and the more indifferent Beebe was to his advances, the more Conway wanted into the deal. To explain the dance between the entrepreneur and potential financial suitors, Beebe drew an analogy to dating. "The more you say no," he said, "the more they seem to want you."

Eventually Beebe relented. Silicon Valley's best-connected angel, it turned out, had a pal among Springfield's syndicate of investors, a relationship Conway used for all its worth. Beebe was concerned with Angel Investors' existing relationship with SmartAge, but recognized the potential power of Conway's network. The only hang-up was that the deadline for closing their second round was upon them, so there wasn't time to show Conway their basic presentation. So Angel Investors ended up buying into the Springfield Project based on a cryptic two-line description of Beebe's business.

The much-vaunted West Coast way of doing business in the late 1990s generally encouraged people to appear hungry enough so that others took you seriously but not so hungry that they noticed how hungry you truly were. Conway, in contrast, puffed with pride when recalling the tenacity he displayed getting into the Springfield Project, now called Bigstep.com. "I'm very aggressive when I need to be," Conway says with a nonchalant shrug. "If I decide I want something to happen and I'm very motivated, I try *real* hard to make it happen." The more competitive the deal, the harder Conway fought to get in. From his front-row seat, Bozeman declared Conway "the premier elbow guy in the business."

———

History teaches us that the country saw the creation of more than three thousand automobile startups between 1900 and 1925, "turning out all manner of cars, from three-wheel models to ones steered by ship-like tillers," according to an article in *The New York Times.* Three survived to the modern era. More recently, the PC revolution gave rise to so many promising companies that would in short order fade from memory: Commodore, Kaypro, Digital Research, to name just a few. Another example is the disk storage business, a lucrative field through much of the past twenty years, but not so lucrative that the sector could support the twenty or so companies that in the early 1980s promised to capture at least a 30 percent share of the market.

But who had time to consult history when there was hardly time to take a leak?

Life during the Internet's first wave, when the majority of Internet entrepreneurs were nerds cranking out code because they were gripped by the notion they were creating something cool, was intense, but as out-of-control and hectic as life might have felt then, the second wave was that much more all-consuming. Life in 1997, says Sparkpr's Donna Sokolsky, was almost manageable. She'd work from eight in the morning till nine at night, maybe meet a friend for dinner or a glass of wine, and fall asleep by midnight. By 1999, though, she was typically at the office by six A.M. and routinely stayed there until midnight. There was no more time for casual dinners with friends or leisurely glasses of wine, at least not during the week.

By the start of 1999, the MBAs had shoved the geeks aside. There were many exceptions, of course, but the MBAs generally displayed no more interest in a product's or service's underlying technologies than the corporate raiders of the 1980s showed in the businesses they took over and then broke apart for a quick profit. For the typical MBA arriving in Silicon Valley in the late 1990s, the Internet was a fairy-tale land disembodied from reality, where creativity meant flipping through the yellow pages in search of inspiration—flowers on the Net! Hardware! Pet food! (Hell, how creative had Amazon's Jeff Bezos been—books on the Internet.) Jeff Bonforte, the technology-minded founder behind an online data storage startup called I-drive.com, laughed at himself for the $1,000 or so he blew in mid-1999 attending something called "Bootcamp for Startups," sponsored by Garage.com. The event reminded Bonforte of one of those get-rich-quick seminars led by someone claiming to have made millions in the real estate game with no money down. He sat in a cavernous room crammed with more than five hundred people, and almost everyone he met was a recent MBA desperate for an Internet grub stake. The featured guest was Steve Jurvetson, a big-name VC who had been recently profiled in *The New York Times Magazine*. Whenever Jurvetson said anything, no matter how inane ("If you can't communicate your idea in no more than ten PowerPoint slides, then you don't have an interesting idea"), people around him pulled out their Cross pens and scribbled down his pearls, as if Moses were handing down the Ten Commandments. At one point, members of the audience were invited to pitch their ideas to Jurvetson and several other VCs. It was *The Gong Show* meets the Internet. Participants were granted sixty seconds to pitch their idea, but most were hit with a thumbs-down well before their time expired. Bonforte described the day as "an absurd window into how the Valley was becoming this magnet for every MBA and his brother wanting to get rich," a world in which "technology didn't matter."

The media thrilled over every element of the story. The preposterous and exciting happening called the Internet IPO was a staple of the feature pages, and before long each one sounded more or less the same: the early jitters of the road shows, the limousines and private jets, the obligatory pitched arguments over pricing before everyone walked away rich. "Exhausted yet elated," NeverHeardaUs.com CEO Lowden Rich says with a grin when he sees his company's Nasdaq symbol scroll across the ticker for the first time. Cheers go up, people sip $100-a-bottle Dom Pérignon from plastic cups. Cofounders were worth $200 million each by day's end, unless they were worth a billion. Yahoo paid $4 billion for GeoCities, which wasn't so much a business as it was a venue for anyone wanting to post a website without paying for one, and $6 billion for Broadcast.com, which allowed Yahoo to get into the anything but profitable online television business. The papers reported on orange-haired twenty-four-year-olds with multiple pierces and a net worth north of $10 million, and all those senior vice presidents at old-line companies who left behind secure sinecures for a few hundred thousand options in a dot-com they hoped would make them imponderably rich. Every golden moment was magnified and glorified, prompting hordes more to buy one-way tickets to San Francisco. A paper worth in the seven figures seemed as if it were just a matter of showing up.

By 1999, the Valley's infrastructure was groaning under its own weight and in danger of toppling in on itself, but few who were part of that world seemed to pause long enough to notice. The area's waitresses, janitors, and day care workers had long ago moved to faraway places because of the spike in rents, but by 1999 the Valley's teachers, its cops, and even Stanford profs were feeling priced out. So many startups were vying for the same small set of lawyers that attorneys who catered to venture-backed new companies held tryouts, sifting through business plans, agreeing to represent only the most promising teams. Among the chosen it wasn't enough to pay an attorney's exorbitant hourly rates; by 1999 it was a given a firm would demand a cut of equity. Hiring a PR agency proved equally exasperating. Her firm, Donna Sokolsky says, received as many as forty unsolicited phone calls a week requesting their services, yet they never handled more than maybe eight clients at a time. Sparkpr, like virtually every other well-regarded PR firm, also required options from every company it represented and therefore chose to work only with those companies it concluded had the best chance of going public. Advertising agencies, executive headhunters, consultants of all stripes, even landlords once office space grew as scarce as qualified Java programmers—anyone who could finagled a piece of the action.

Nowhere was the feeding frenzy more intense than on the lower end of the fundraising food chain, where Angel Investors competed with new creations of every form and size. In 1998, the "Internet incubator" became the hot idea du jour. The incubator was another device for grabbing equity in nascent Internet startups. An incubator's host offered less experienced entrepreneurs office space and ostensibly wisdom in exchange for a cut of the action. It was a relatively cheap and easy way to collect shares in a diversified set of potentially lucrative deals, so everywhere around the Bay Area old hands and even a fair share of puppies who had no business advising anyone on anything were renting office suites that they then chopped into mazelike warrens of smaller offices populated by baby startups hoping to grow successful enough to mandate that they find a larger space. By mid-1999, Internet-oriented incubators numbered in the hundreds. Even some venture firms, tired of paying the steep premiums attached to a company because it had already been discovered by an angel or an incubator entrepreneur, established their own incubators. So-called matchmaker firms such as Angeltips.com and Garage.com were another new creation on the scene. The matchmakers were the entrepreneurial equivalent of video dating. They promised to hook startups up with a wide wide world of potential funders—in exchange for a hefty fee and of course shares.

The more money that poured into the Valley, the more the ranks of the venture capitalists swelled. Where there were 397 venture firms in 1995, according to the National Venture Capital Association, by 2000 their ranks had grown by 75 percent, to 693. Baby-faced, hypercompetitive VCs rushed around the Valley attempting to justify annual salaries in the many hundreds of thousands, not to mention a share of the profits. The presence of so many newcomers created what the venture capitalist Neil Weintraut described as "an incredibly competitive environment" in which everyone was cordial to one another except "when we were tearing each other's eyes out." The two-month due-diligence cycle that had collapsed to one month or less with the Internet was now sometimes something to be done after the fact. "If a deal was hot enough," Weintraut says, "you locked the door and didn't let the founders out until they had at least verbally committed to a deal." Thinking about an idea even overnight might have meant someone else snapped up that company.

"We all did due diligence, or at least the major VCs did," says Weintraut, who co-invested with Angel Investors on several deals. "The real issue is that we realized once it was too late that we forgot to pay attention to this one important factor called profitability." Such a statement is akin to a pro scout proclaiming that a player has all the intangibles to become a starter in the NBA except dribbling and shooting.

It was against this backdrop that Conway and Bozeman sought to own pieces of the Valley's choicest startups before they were discovered by the competition. Dotcast CEO Dave Atkinson is a Conway drinking buddy who is grateful for the millions Angel Investors poured into his company. But he believes his friend fell under the same spell that bewitched so many investors in the second half of 1999. If you ask someone in the Valley to name the category most emblematic of the era's embrace of lamebrain ideas, the likely answer is online pet stores; hundreds of millions were invested in a quartet of them. Atkinson is no exception. By the time the online pet store wars began, it was obvious that shipping even books and CDs was prohibitively expensive, let alone forty-pound bags of dog chow or twenty-four-can boxes of cat food. But it was as if no one among a prestigious list of investors in any of the high-profile online pet store startups ever thought to do the math, Conway among them as an investor in Petopia.

"Entrepreneurs could stand with buckets at the bottom of Sand Hill Road scooping up the money that was flowing down," Atkinson says. "So what you saw were many companies funded that should never have been considered even for a second. It was unconscionable to fund ideas with no business model, but there was this belief that if they spent enough money building the brand, then it would translate into a big business." *Any* company seeking to build a business around pet supplies, and also sports, Atkinson says, should have been suspect. Conway was an early investor not only in Petopia, but in a long list of sports-oriented sites, including ZuluSports, Pupuple Sports, LevelEdge, and Digital Media Campus. "That's the nature of mass euphoria, or a mass hysteria, or whatever you want to call it," Atkinson says.

An investors' list as wired as Conway's could pass along word of the hottest deals, but they also tended to be far more astute students of the Internet than anyone running Angel Investors. Occasionally one of Conway's plugged-in investors would peruse the list of companies added to the Angel Investors portfolio and think, "They funded *that*?" For one investor, a list of Conway's worst picks would have to include AllAdvantage, a company that paid people to look at ads over the Internet (the company quickly figured out it was paying out more to members than it could attract from advertisers), and Backflip, a company with a great product (an online bookmark) but no real plan for making money on this service they gave away for free. A second investor found herself laughing over Angel Investors' decision to invest in Evite—until she realized that some of *her* money was in this free online invitation service that lost more money the more successful it became. Investors would read through capsule descriptions of the

Angel portfolio and they didn't know whether to laugh or cry. There was 12degrees, a website that allowed you to arrange "customized foreign vacations," and SuperSig, a software product for those wanting to create a customized e-mail signature. There was, too, Asimba ("Because endorphins feel good"), a website for those seeking training and weight loss programs; AskForFree.com, which answered people's questions over the Internet *for free;* and ePlast.com, which, in its short life, aimed to become the world's leading marketplace for the resins that serve as the raw material for plastics. Would any of these lead to a business offering the kind of payoffs the venture capitalists were seeking?

Some grew nervous about the fate of their money the more they learned about Angel Investors' picks. Others, however, were impressed by Conway's picking ability, despite some of his more sublime choices. Conway was still an Internet neophyte. One of his assistants still printed out his e-mails, and typed out and sent his handwritten replies. Any time Conway might have spent on the World Wide Web was likely to have occurred with someone standing at his side, if not sitting at the keyboard. And yet those around him were amazed by his eye for spotting popular next-generation technologies, if not breakthroughs that would ultimately prove profitable. "In hindsight, Ron obviously made some investments way too rapidly," says investor Joe Beninato. "There were some questionable investments. But, with that said, a lot of very good investments have come out of this rapid-fire approach." I-drive's Jeff Bonforte is not an investor in either Angel-I or Angel-II, nor has his company received funding from Conway, but he looked over Conway's list of investments and was impressed, especially with his more technology-oriented bets. He was shocked when told Conway was something of a Luddite. Sure Conway got "caught up in the hype plays," but to him Conway has a much better eye than many venture capitalists purported to be industry soothsayers.

"In the middle of the bubble," says Jennifer Bailey, now an executive with MyCFO, "the criterion for success was unpredictable and changing all the time. You had a company like Amazon that can

ꞬꞬꞬꞬꞬ the way it did without ever having to forecast a time when they'd be profitable. So who could say with certainty what investments made sense at the time and which didn't?"

—

One observer likened Conway's investment style to a "drive-by shooting using a shotgun." Conway allowed that he's impatient and has adopted an investment style that reflects his temperament. He believes in first impressions: if minutes into a meeting he's feeling excited, he's likely to invest, especially if a startup has been endorsed by someone part of his network. If not, there's little hope he'll ever back that venture. He confesses, too, there were times he knew he'd be investing in a company even before meeting an entrepreneur and hearing his or her idea. He mentions two former Netscape executives whom he considered two of his better sources for news about hot new startups, Ram Shriram and his close friend Mike Homer. "If Mike or Ram tell me, 'I'm putting in half a million dollars, I'm committed, are you?' I would say, 'We're probably going to do the deal, when can I meet the entrepreneur?' " Pat Burns, co-founder of a company called Demandline, phoned Conway in mid-1999 to tell him about the business-to-business exchange that he and his partner had built to cater to small businesses. "He jumped on it immediately," Burns told the trade publication *ComputerUser.com*. "The next morning we had our money: the $700,000 seed money."

Bozeman bristles at the suggestion that Angel Investors deserved to be lumped in with a class of investors he dubbed "drive-by VCs." Angel Investors turned away somewhere between seven thousand and eight thousand deals by Bozeman's calculations: how, then, can anyone suggest they were an easy mark? "We're very interested in quality," he says. Still, Bozeman confesses that sometimes the prevailing mood got the better of them, Conway especially. "The class of errors we made were because Ron felt it was so hot he thought he had to jump in," Bozeman says, adding, "The strikeouts are unfortunately part of this business."

On Sand Hill Road, every partner is typically heard from before a venture firm commits money. Some stick to an ironclad rule that dictates that they will invest only if the vote is unanimous. But Angel Investors is more an extension of Conway than a true partnership. The agreement between Bozeman and Conway allowed either of them to pull the trigger on a deal without the other's okay, though neither recalls a deal that Bozeman chose to fund unilaterally. But Bozeman had no trouble naming deals he learned about only after Conway had approved them. "These are deals that I'd probably say would've benefited from having multiple views, but I'm not sure the froth would allow that at the time," Bozeman says.

Hero Capital was a company hatched in the hopes they could create an online market in which people traded not equity in corporations but shares in the careers of athletes, actors, and eventually twenty-two-year-olds without the resources to attend medical school. If what one might call the MD-to-Be Exchange is ever up and running, stock in a kid with perfect MCATs would have a much higher worth than stock in one who attended med school in Grenada, because whatever percentage of her future earnings the MCAT ace put up for sale would presumably be worth far more than that of the prospective doctor who was forced to travel overseas for his schooling. Hero Capital was peddling one of those cockamamy ideas so bold and audacious that in 1999, at the height of the frenzy, it seemed a perfectly reasonable way to spend a few hundred thousand dollars and maybe earn back twenty times your initial investment. It was also a startup that even Bozeman pegged a likely loser, despite the million dollars Angel Investors sank into the company.

"That's one on which I didn't have veto power," Bozeman says with a hearty laugh. "That's Ron's deal. I hate to say it that way, but that's not a deal I would have chosen to do on my own." So why did Conway end up doing it? "What you need to understand about Hero Capital is that it's a Mike Homer deal," Bozeman says. "And Ron has *huge* respect for Mike Homer." As Bozeman tells it, Homer had already helped Conway land a piece of several hot deals. He owed Homer one.

Bozeman described Candybarrel.com as another "Ron deal," though later, after talking with Conway, he would say he had remembered wrong and *he* deserved the blame or credit. In any event, Angel Investors' motives for doing the deal were also rooted more in loyalty and obligation than the inherent brilliance of the idea. Candybarrel was an online exchange aiming to hook up candy makers with candy wholesalers and candy retailers—a one-stop electronic shop for all your candy fulfillment needs. The Candybarrel business plan noted that the candy, nut, and snack market is a $140 billion a year business, but it was still a pretty narrow niche and it wasn't clear the industry saw a pressing need to conduct its business over the Internet with some newly minted West Coast company. When Bozeman first learned of Candybarrel at the end of 1999, he was incredulous. "You look at the business and you go, 'Why would anyone want to invest in this?' " Bozeman says. But Candybarrel had come to Bozeman and Conway via Angel-II investor Fred Sibayan, one of the brains behind a publicly traded company called Exodus Communications.

"Fred is a brilliant guy who was putting in a lot of energy and a lot of money into Candybarrel," Bozeman says. "We did [the Candybarrel deal] as part of the allegiance to lend our support to three other deals he had brought to us."

Yes, but do Tiger, Arnold, and Shaq want to hear that Angel Investors put a few hundred thousand dollars into a company because essentially Angel Investors owed its best-known benefactor one? Bozeman answered that question by noting that Shaq has benefited from that tendency. He describes Dunk.net, Shaq's website, as "another one of those deals I was vetoing," but Conway always seemed a soft touch for flashy, celebrity-endorsed Internet companies out of Los Angeles. Dunk.net had already received $30 million from Technology Crossover Ventures (TCV), one of the venture world's heavier hitters, and though theoretically an angel fund invests only in companies that have yet to raise serious outside funding, Conway believed in following the smart money whenever given a chance. So Conway threw in $500,000 from Angel-II. "Ron will generally not give a shit if it's a good deal or not if investors he respects have already invested," Bozeman says, and TCV is "a very big, well-regarded firm." Besides, what's half a million when you're sitting on a $180 million mound of money?

Chapter 5

—

COME TO JESUS

By the spring of 2000, everything was going pretty much as Conway had hoped it would when he first dreamed up Angel Investors. The most sought-after venture capitalists were investing in his startups. That meant that all these companies he had valued at maybe $10 million were suddenly worth in the tens of millions, magically turning all these $250,000 and $500,000 commitments into investments worth in the many millions, at least on paper. By March, more than a dozen of his portfolio companies—companies in which Angel Investors typically owned a 2 to 5 percent share—had filed with the Securities and Exchange Commission to go public, and many more were meeting with the top investment bankers to discuss their own prospects for an IPO.

And then—poof.

—

The good times weren't all good times, of course. Conway was working morning, noon, and night, as was his loyal sidekick Robin, yet there were constant complaints that the two of them weren't

doing enough, Conway especially, to help the Angel Investors portfolio companies. Entrepreneurs complaining that their angels and
VCs were shortchanging them in favor of the quest for the next hot
deal was the Valley equivalent of grousing about the weather, but the
surprise was that people were saying it about Conway. Sure, people
bitched about the two reclusive engineers who started an incubator
called Venture Frogs after selling their company to Microsoft for a
couple of hundred million. No one would accuse either of being
glad-handers, and neither had much in the way of connections if you
discounted their participation in Angel Investors.

"Conway had like the world's largest Rolodex, but the criticism
about Angel Investors was the same as about Venture Frogs, that
they were not doing nearly enough for their portfolio companies,"
says Jad Duwaik, a San Francisco–based entrepreneur who occasionally hosted salons for Internet entrepreneurs through an organization he called Greenhouse for Startups. Conway didn't disagree
with Duwaik's assessment of Angel Investors. He was so busy raising Angel-II in the fall of 1999 while simultaneously chasing hot
new deals that he knew he was shortchanging this aspect of the job.
That's why in January 2000 he hired someone full-time to, as he
said it, "leverage his Rolodex."

By that point, Conway had already hired several more staffers,
including a third partner, a money manager from Barclays Bank
named Fred Grauer. That was in October 1999, by which time a
long list of high-profile executives had jumped from long-held secure posts to dot-coms, yet even *The New York Times* took note of
the Grauer hire, a defection that reporter Steve Lohr declared a
"vivid illustration" of "the changes that the Internet gold rush has
brought." Grauer had headed the $575 billion Barclays Global In-
vestors funds, and though he would last only a year with Angel Investors, he enthused in an interview a couple of months after he
was hired, "The pace, everything, is so exciting—living on the
edge of the envelope!" Conway and Grauer were from entirely different work worlds, but naturally there was a strong prior connection. They had met years earlier during a fundraising drive at the

private school their children attended, and Grauer was already an Angel investor.

When you're Ron Conway, you don't place an ad in the newspaper or even post a classified on a website once you've decided to hire someone. You instead start flipping through the Rolodex. He stopped at H when he got to Margot Hirsch, an old family friend who was both a close friend of his wife's and a former work colleague of Conway's. Hirsch worked for him in sales at Altos, and then half a dozen years later Conway convinced her to join him at Personal Training Systems.

Hirsch didn't need much persuading. She was an investor in Angel-I, so she already had a stake in the fund's success. She also knew better than to think she could say no to Conway, despite an intimate understanding of what he'd expect of her. "Ron works his fingers to the bone and holds those under him to the same standard," she says. Fashionwise, Conway and Bozeman preferred the standard uniform worn by the Valley's money men, slacks and dress shirts without ties or sports jackets. Hirsch, who was forty years old at the start of 2000, is well coifed and East Coast professional, a woman who fancies tailored red business suits, colorful silk scarves, pearl earrings, and French-tipped manicured nails.

Officially, Hirsch serves as Angel's director of business development—in Valleyspeak, its director of "biz dev." In reality, however, that's not much of a post inside Angel Investors. "Basically head of business development is a fancy way of saying I'm one of Ron's assistants," she says. Her main job is helping the Angel portfolio companies secure deals with larger, more established companies, especially those with ties to Conway. "We make sure that a proposal isn't buried in a stack on the right person's desk," Hirsch says. "We make sure it's on top of the pile."

It's Hirsch's job to hassle Angel's 550 investors so they help the fund's portfolio companies. Let's say the CEO of AnotherStupidIdea.com seeks a meeting with a key decision maker inside Amazon.com. Maybe they hope to sell a product on the Amazon website, or maybe they're peddling a nifty technology that Amazon might want to use. No problem, Hirsch says; "A lot of guys at Amazon are investors." She mentions her main contact at Amazon (an investor, of course), a top executive who is always "sweet enough" to lend a hand to the company in question. "They don't necessarily get the deal," Hirsch says, "but at least they are always granted a meeting." Rarely does Hirsch come up empty when seeking an inside contact at a crucial Internet company. Conway's list of investors includes at least three people connected to Yahoo, eBay, AOL, Intel, Compaq, Microsoft, and Cisco, among other companies.

So what if investors who double as top executives are presented with an ethical quandary every time Hirsch phones them? Earlier Hirsch had mentioned an Angel investor named Mike Volpi, who, as a Cisco senior vice president and the company's chief strategy officer, is a man any entrepreneur working in Cisco's orbit wants to know. Mike is such a nice man, Hirsch says. Think of the volume of e-mail he must receive. So busy, yet he has faithfully responded to every one of her e-mails within twenty-four hours. Hirsch dismisses as unlikely the suggestion that he's motivated less by manners and more by the fact that he has a personal financial stake in the fund. "I think Mike wears his Cisco hat more than his investor hat," Hirsch says. "I don't think he's thinking much about his investment." As a top Cisco employee who has been with the networking giant since 1994, Volpi's net worth undoubtedly stands in the many millions. Volpi notes that Cisco allows its executives to invest in venture funds, and Angel Investors is a venture firm, "so it is consistent with Cisco's policy." He assures me that if he ever perceived a conflict of interest between Cisco and an Angel company (so far he has not), "I would act accordingly." Yet he's also a longtime member of the Valley elite, and he understands the expectations that fall upon you when you're part of the club. If you say yes when opportunity knocks, you're expected to play the game by the established rules.

"We never push it," Hirsch says, stressing she'll never ask an investor for anything but an introduction and a good word where appropriate. Apparently, Conway isn't nearly as dainty. He'd see an investor at a cocktail party, Hirsch says, and remember that he hadn't responded to an e-mail someone with Angel Investors had sent two months earlier. "We never heard back from you," he'd say. "What's going on?" Hirsch wonders which is the more amazing fact, that her boss acted that brashly when talking with the likes of a Marc Andreessen or that he remembered that an e-mail sent two months earlier had gone unanswered. Not for a moment did it strike her that her boss was blurring any ethical lines.

"If I want to know the gentlemen's rules in a certain situation, I know all I have to do is call Ron," says Vividence's Artie Wu, who describes Conway as an "informal keeper of the rule book." If so, then the Valley is intimate and incestuous, a cozy world in which everyone is friends with everyone else—and of course friends do favors for one another, especially when a favor means everyone gets a little richer. In the Valley, using an executive's post to make a bundle on the side is a long-standing tradition, as much a part of the local ethic as celebrating the obliteration of a personal life as an evolution to some higher plane that entwines work and play. Yet Conway systemized this practice when he put together Angel Investors.

There were many advances on this front during the Internet years, no surprise given all the money that was at stake. Consider the advisory board, a fixture of the Internet scene. The clued-in Internet entrepreneur understood that an advisory board was the fastest, easiest way to buy instant connections to established companies, especially those targeted as potential customers or partners. The Valley's advisory boards were stacked with well-placed executives who loaned their names to companies in exchange for equity stakes. Some larger companies prohibited such arrangements, but most did not, even when (as invariably happened) the startup sought a business arrangement with the advisory board member's company. An executive typically "recused" himself from a decision on a deal with a business in which he owned stock, but before doing so he typically would have chaperoned the startup inside the door, made the proper introductions, and left his underlings to feel the lingering pressures inherent when learning that one of the big bosses has a vested interest in a deal. One participant spoke of his half-dozen advisory board posts as if it was a diversified investment strategy. "You have six of these going at once and the chances of a big payoff are pretty good," he says.

Inside Angel Investors they dubbed it keiretsu, borrowing the phrase popularized by Kleiner Perkins five years earlier. It was a fancy way to say that Conway has formalized standard operating procedure in the Valley, where favors are traded freely and people are accustomed to wearing more than one hat while working on a single transaction. Every company in which Conway has invested, or so it seems, has withdrawn at least a favor or two from his favor bank. He helped Andreessen's Loudcloud secure a meeting at Williams-Sonoma (an executive from that chain of upscale kitchen stores is an Angel investor), he helped a promising young company called Yodlee gain a meeting with a large, New York–based financial institution, phoning one of Angel's investors, who was a top executive at that bank. "The decision [to partner up with Yodlee] was made at another level, but the request to take a look at the product came from high up, and that helped tremendously," says Ram Shriram, who sits on Yodlee's board of directors. "Not many starts get that kind of break. It's up to the startup to perform if it's going to make the deal, but that introduction meant everything."

It was all cozy, sometimes too cozy from the perspective of those inside the fund. Conway had invested in any number of overlapping businesses, including several online music companies and a long list of competing b-to-b's. Complicating matters further, Conway invited some of his favorite founders from Angel-I to invest in Angel-II, including Bigstep's Andrew Beebe and SmartAge's Bill Lohse. Bigstep and SmartAge competed head-to-head (along with at least two other companies inside Angel Investors), so the two of them were invariably running into each other at conferences and other industry events. So Beebe would see Lohse and say, "Hey, I'm one of your investors." And Lohse would be like, "And I'm one of yours!" It was a cute joke that passed between them that was one part clever, two parts weird, and entirely Silicon Valley.

—

How did you get above the noise at the peak of the frenzy when so many companies were vying for the attention of the press and the venture capitalists? Conway might not have been the most discriminating of investors, but in short order an endorsement by Angel Investors would be widely viewed as an important early endorsement that might win a startup a more serious look, no small leg up with thousands of young companies all descending on the same small set of business publications and venture capitalists. In the Valley they called it the halo effect: a company flashed the names of its top-drawer backers in the hopes that their pedigrees would impress the press and the VCs, but also the lawyers and PR firms and others suddenly in hot demand in an ecosystem overwhelmed by too many startups.

Conway periodically showed up at the offices of the *Red Herring* to meet with Chris Alden, the magazine's editorial director. Alden is an investor in both Angel-I and Angel-II, and Conway, an investor in the *Herring,* sits on the magazine's board of directors. (I wrote this book while in the employ of *The Industry Standard,* a *Herring* competitor.) Inevitably, a magazine like the *Herring,* which covered the startup scene, would report on some of the portfolio's two-hundred-plus companies, but rather than cautiously shying away from the appearances of a conflict of interest, Conway bulled ahead, selling hard whatever companies he thought deserved attention. He pitched his companies to Alden, and then he would walk down the hall to hand to the magazine's day-to-day editor, Jason Pontin, "a folder with one-pagers about all our new companies." Conway would grow frustrated that the *Herring* often failed to write about portfolio companies he believed to be worthy of attention, but it certainly wasn't for a lack of effort on his part. One former *Herring* staffer said that Conway's regular visits to their office called to mind a guy on the street flashing open his trench coat to reveal the many watches he has for sale: surely at least one must interest you.

Angel Investors proved something of a one-stop, full-service adviser, helping fledgling companies with a laundry list of incidentals, from making introductions at the Silicon Valley Bank to putting in a good word with an experienced accounting firm. Conway or Bozeman was always meeting with their portfolio CEOs at one of their lunchtime offices up and down the peninsula. The two are a pragmatic pair with more than fifty years of experience between them, and both seem to share the same gift for communicating unpleasant truths in such a way that those on the receiving end don't walk away feeling beat up or burned. "They'll tell you things like, 'Here's who you need to hire, here's where you're weak, here's where you're going wrong,' " says Maclen Marvit, the co-founder of an Angel-backed e-mail security firm called Disappearing Inc. "They're not the kind for pontificating from up high."

Marvit usually sat across a table from Bozeman. "Bob would come at a moment's notice, but it's not like he'd be in my shorts trying to run my business," Marvit says in a way that strongly suggests that others in his orbit tried to do just that. When he needed to negotiate a deal with an important prospective partner, Bozeman would walk him through the potential pitfalls. "He knows what's on the other side of the mountain I'm about to climb," Marvit says. "I haven't always liked what they've had to say, especially when they're telling me that I'm wrong. I haven't always listened. But goddamn them if they're not always right."

Conway's connections proved especially important when his startups sought a next round of venture capital. For years Conway had been collecting contacts among the Valley's money men, starting in 1985 after he left Altos Computer for the first time. His work as a consultant to PC software companies caused him to make the acquaintance of venture capitalists up and down Sand Hill Road. Three children attending a private school at the Menlo Park–Atherton border helped Conway to both deepen existing relationships and make new friends among those VCs who also had children. He was invited to participate in some of the most prized side funds, and through events at the school (he was one of the school's most active fundraisers), he socialized with many of the industry's rising stars. Conway calculates that by the time he started Angel Investors, he was on a first-name basis with well over one hundred VCs.

Conway's connections didn't guarantee that a company would receive venture funding, but they at least meant that some of the area's most highly regarded VCs would take a hard look. Conway's reputation among the established VCs is mixed—some are inclined to see him as an amateur playing a professional's game—but even those inclined to view him as an easy mark recognized there was no one better at sniffing out the next hot company. Their reputations as bold seers notwithstanding, most VCs tended to want outside validation before placing a bet on an unproven company. Even most of the top VCs in the business seriously entertained a proposal only if it had been already endorsed by someone inside their world. Conway was a test that had been passed and a relationship that needed to be honored. Not surprisingly, roughly three in every four startups receiving financing through Angel-I were funded by what Conway deemed a top-tier VC.

Yet by early 2000, when Angel-II companies started seeking meetings to discuss future funding, the top VCs were no longer nearly as eager to meet with a Conway-backed company. By that point, Sand Hill had had more than its fill of dot-coms, especially those focused on the consumer market, but Bozeman was inclined to believe the top VCs were simply overwhelmed with work. "The top guys didn't have the bandwidth to handle all we were throwing at them," he says. It was time for Conway to make new friends. Each day he perused VentureWire with an eye out for any new hires, especially at well-established firms. He would phone to offer his congratulations and, after determining the new hire's area of expertise, started selling the appropriate companies. "We'd be all over that VC for the next six months," Conway explains. "We figured that they didn't have the deal flow yet and that they'd be anxious to earn a reputation. Our goal was our portfolio companies sitting with them twenty-four hours a day, seven days a week, so they had no time to meet with anyone else." With time, Conway would seek new friends even among the B-list VCs, filling his calendar with breakfasts at Buck's and lunches wherever a VC might be willing to meet him.

All things considered, the typical angel preferred to invest in a startup and then retire to their beachfront hideaway until it was time to collect their million dollars. They might call a few VCs they considered friends, but that would be about it. Conway, in contrast, shook the money tree on behalf of his portfolio companies, at least those that still ranked among his favorites, with the perseverance of a hacker attempting to shut down a website with a denial-of-service attack. He staged VC workshops for his portfolio companies, his staff prepared thick briefing books listing the name of every partner at the hundreds of venture capital firms that specialize in technology, along with phone numbers, e-mail addresses, and a dossier of companies funded. He beseeched entrepreneurs to approach the task of raising money as if they were Woodward and Bernstein going after a president. List the name of every VC you or anyone inside your company has ever met, he counseled. Then figure out who you know who might also know that VC and go after them. All that you've heard about the Valley being a meritocracy where a good idea is all you need? he would ask them. Forget it. "Pedigree is everything," he said. And for those who didn't have connections of their own to play, he did. "If you need to reach a certain VC, we'll do what we have to to nail him to the ground to make it happen," he told his entrepreneurs. He hassled them until they agreed to perform dry runs, and he drilled them on their thirty-second elevator pitch: Yahoo co-founder Jerry Yang steps on the elevator at the sixth floor, you have until the first floor to inspire his interest in your company—go.

But Conway's counsel and advice didn't count half as much as what he euphemistically calls "creative back channeling." He adopted a methodical approach to his cajoling and arm twisting, instructing the Angel staff to produce regular status sheets so he knew which VCs to approach when. "Have you met with Artie Wu?" he casually asked a VC, though he knew the two had met the previous

Thursday at two P.M., and then slipped in that Wu was meeting with three other VCs, all of whom were of course extremely interested, no matter what the reality. At times he was subtle, at other times he was a guided missile seeking its target. "Will, I'll kick your ass, you're holding up funding," he joshed with Will Hearst III, a venture capitalist at Kleiner Perkins since 1995, at the firm's Christmas party. He showed up wherever VCs were known to gather—to schmooze with them, to glad-hand, and to make good-natured threats to those standing in the way of a company's success.

When a company received its next round of venture funding, Conway typically stepped into the background, even when he invested in further rounds. Even the most devoted father can't parent two hundred companies simultaneously, and even the friendliest VC might resent Conway's heavy hand. Yet it's not like Conway to completely abandon his favorites. "I still get calls from Ron at least every month or two," Wu says, though his firm had hit the venture lottery by securing funding from Kleiner Perkins and Sequoia, perhaps Sand Hill Road's two most respected venture firms. Conway for instance knew Wu was looking for a personnel director to handle the company's explosive hiring binge, so when he learned that a top human resources executive was looking to change jobs, Conway elbowed his way into the competition, winning Wu a meeting with a woman who would become his new "Vice President of People."

"It's not in his contract, so to speak, that he keeps helping you," Wu says. "But he does because he loves the action. He loves seeing deals get done, he loves seeing an idea really happen." Other members of the clan, however, might be forgiven any resentments over the traits one of the prodigal sons chose to underline. The Nasdaq was well into its precipitous decline when Wu uttered these words, and the nature of hard times is that they force difficult choices that families don't have to confront when times are flush.

—

The first big dip in the Nasdaq hit on a Monday in mid-March. The Nasdaq composite index fell nearly 3 percent and then lost another

4 percentage points the next day. People shrugged. It had taken the Nasdaq a mere eighteen weeks to cross the 4,000 mark after reaching 3,000, and then only another ten weeks to cross 5,000. The bright boys paused long enough from their self-satisfied dismissals of "dinosaurs" such as Kmart and Walgreens and The New York Times to makes jokes about people being tired from sprinting for too long. The Nasdaq composite had fallen by more than 10 percentage points for the week, but that was the third 10-percent-plus drop in as many months, and in the first two instances the Nasdaq had roared back.

The Nasdaq continued to slide over the next two weeks, but few seemed to suspect that this was the Big One. During the last week in March, the Nasdaq experienced the third- and fifth-largest point drops in its thirty-year history, falling another 8 percentage points in two days, but mainly the analysts and investment bankers focused on the short-term impact the Nasdaq's decline would have on the many IPOs in the pipeline. The consensus held that most would need to delay their public offerings a few months, until the market settled down. In mid-1998, when the markets were hit by the so-called Asian flu, the Nasdaq fell by 30 percentage points in ten weeks, yet closed up 40 percent for the year. There were steep drops in 1999 as well, a year that saw the Nasdaq rise by another 86 percentage points. The latest gyrations seemed like little more than a brief blip on the race to another set of record highs.

April was a lot like March, except worse. The Nasdaq fell 8 percent on the first trading day of the month, or 349 points, which represented the largest one-day drop in Nasdaq history. On April 2 the composite plummeted 574 points, or by nearly 14 percent (the Nasdaq fell by more than 11 percent on October 19, 1987, so-called Black Monday), but rallied before the final bell to close down only 75 points for the day. The following week obliterated any hope that the dramatic rebound on April 2 represented some kind of bottom in the market. The composite fell by almost a thousand points that week, and more dates were etched into the record books: in a single week, the Nasdaq experienced its three worst point drops in its history, culminating with a record-setting 355-point drop on April 14. The Nasdaq composite had fallen 34 percent from its March 10 high.

"The biggest bull market in Nasdaq history," Floyd Norris of *The New York Times* wrote, "has given way to the fastest growing bear market ever."

The numbers were worse still if viewed strictly from the perspective of Internet companies that had recently gone public. A long list of Internet companies tumbled by 80 percent or more, including eToys (down 93 percent from its high), Drkoop.com (down 94 percent), and the retailer Beyond.com (down 91 percent). The future promised many more steep declines. An analyst at Sanford C. Bernstein & Co. found that only one in four companies that had gone public in the previous six months was profitable, yet now investors were expressing a clear unwillingness to accept the promise of profits at some unspecified future date. For so long the digerati had triumphantly ballyhooed the "Internet speed" at which the economy was being transformed, yet the best evidence offered to date portended the expeditious end of the dot-com revolution in one month's time.

The pundits and other talking heads—at least those who hadn't gone suddenly radio silent—struggled gamely to put the best spin on things. Among the investment bankers the favored term for what had just occurred was "hiccup"—and of course whatever was happening was something they had been anticipating. The entrepreneurial set, even those at top companies whose stocks were trading at one fifth their highs, declared the market's decline a positive development. It's as if all of them had decided at once that the cliché of the moment would be a farm metaphor: these hard times would separate the wheat from the chaff—and we're strictly grade-A wheat. The future still looks bright. Wall Street will reward us when we start posting profits, which should be sometime over the next four quarters. The Valley's vaunted confidence still reigned. A one-third drop in the stock market could ruin your day in Silicon Valley, but only if you let it.

Conway could not be counted among those who shrugged off the meltdown as an irritating hiccup that could be overcome by the financial equivalent of gulping a glass of water without taking a breath. He's congenitally optimistic, a man who sees only potential when he stares at someone's barely started masterpiece, yet he's also a grown-up who's been around a long time and a pragmatist who seeks a tidy return on the money he's invested on behalf of 550 people, including himself. He worked his way through a thick stack of business magazines and came away convinced that he could no longer count on quick payouts from infant companies that would go public before they had posted a single profitable quarter. Some experts, though, were predicting that a tightening IPO market would bring about a torrent of mergers in the coming weeks. Conway embraced that prediction as his great hope: the established Internet companies, where his contacts were strong, would buy many of his more promising companies.

The shift in direction wasn't as dramatic as it might have seemed from the outside. Since December, Bozeman had been aggressively pushing Conway to slow down their pace of investing. By that point the top-tier VCs were far more reluctant to spend $5 million for a slice of a company that might or might not prove profitable, and some were already bracing for a fallout among e-commerce sites, the so-called b-to-c's. By February, when the partnership had more than fifty companies simultaneously looking for follow-on funding, Conway finally relented. They would stop slapping down bets as if they were game show contestants racing against a clock. "That was probably the hardest period for Ron," Bozeman says. "We had built the engine to really run at a high pace."

Conway is not a man for halfway measures. In mid-April, on the weekend following the worst point drop in Nasdaq history, he sequestered himself in his home office to write a pair of e-mails. He sent one to his investors list, the other to his portfolio CEOs. In the past, he told both groups, we've preached the wisdom of holding out for the top-tier VCs, but those days are over. He counseled his portfolio CEOs to start the fund-raising cycle sooner rather than later.

Meet with any venture capitalist willing to give you the time of day. The bottom line, he told them, was that the leverage had shifted from the entrepreneurs to the VCs, who wouldn't be shy about exercising the power they had regained. Unless you have stockpiled at least twelve months of cash reserves in the bank, he told his CEOs, you should be "aggressively" thinking about selling to a larger company.

At around that same time Conway hired away an analyst from Credit Suisse First Boston, one of the Valley's better-regarded investment banks, to fill the newly created post of an M&A, or mergers and acquisitions, adviser. Conway started taking meetings with even the third-tier VCs whose phone messages he had never bothered to return in months past. And when he wasn't eating lunch with Joe Smith from Joe Smith Ventures, he was talking to reporters. Conway's name was suddenly everywhere in the media. He was on CNN talking about the wisdom of M&A, his quotes appeared in an array of periodicals ranging from *The Wall Street Journal* to the *National Post* of Canada to the *New York Post*. "Ron," says venture capitalist Lise Buyer, "moved quicker than almost anyone else out there."

Three weeks after sending out his first M&A e-mail, Conway sent out a second. If anything, this one was more forcefully written than the first. He was no longer recommending but ordering. "If you have $10M or less in the bank," he wrote, "you must . . . look at M&A options, especially if your company is in BtoC, content, advertising model, community, commerce, and even BtoB." Roughly 70 percent of his portfolio fell into those categories. He closed by instructing his CEOs that they "must attend our M&A day on May 24th." This was what he later called his "come to Jesus" meeting.

The meeting was held at a hotel by the San Francisco Airport. Selling his new plan with the vigor of an ambitious young salesman working on commission, Conway stacked a panel with entrepreneurs who had ended up fabulously rich after selling their companies. He invited experts so that his CEOs could hear the numbers: in the first three months of 2000, the average price paid for a privately held venture-backed company was $485 million. Besides, every entrepreneur claims that what drives him more than anything else is not the money but a desire to have an impact on the wider world. If the aim is to maximize the number of people using a service or product, each panelist said in his or her own way, who better to help you accomplish that than a well-established company that already has millions of users?

The event began with a Conway speech, delivered in his usual blunt, plainspoken style. We'll no longer be investing more money in many of your companies, he told the assembled CEOs. We predict that as many as ten of you will shut down your companies in the next six months. The rest of you, if you don't want to share that same fate, cut your burn rate by 25 percent. Only the best of you should even be dreaming of an IPO, he said; the rest of you should already be busy flirting with potential suitors. And for God's sake don't make the same mistake as the two Angel companies that had procrastinated thinking about being acquired until they were two payrolls from insolvency, and thus too late to be seeking a white knight.

Conway was out of town when *The Wall Street Journal* phoned to ask about his latest message, so Robin took the call. "You have to hit people with a two-by-four to get their attention," Bozeman told the paper. What he left unsaid, however, is that when you're dealing with brashly self-confident man-child CEOs who've only known life inside the bubble, sometimes not even a two-by-four works.

Chapter 6

—

F***ED COMPANIES

The first Angel Investors company to fold was Violet.com, a site that sold a quirky assortment of goods from orchid-oil lamps to overpriced picture frames. Imagine an online version of a boutique called Hidden Treasures that defied easy explanation, except in this case Violet.com featured a search engine that let shoppers buy gifts based on their mood. The company was co-founded by Amy Barnett, a former Apple Computer engineer and an investor in both Angel-I and Angel-II. Conway had thrown $300,000 into Violet's $3 million first round, in October 1999. By February of 2000, however, according to venture capitalist Neil Weintraut, Violet had already burned through nearly the entire $3 million. By that point Weintraut had sunk far more than $300,000 into Violet, and wasn't about to throw more good money after bad. Conway, however, hoping that a cash infusion would help Violet keep its doors open long enough to find a buyer, invested another $500,000, to no avail. The company officially folded in April 2000.

Two more Angel-II companies, StyleSeek.com and Craft.com, went out of business that spring. Both were online retailers, and they cost Conway & Co. roughly half a million each. Conway was a big believer in consumer-oriented websites, the so-called b-to-c's. With hindsight that would prove a very expensive mistake. "Capital sources were tired of spending tens of millions of dollars on these competing consumer sites to see which company would come out on top," Weintraut says.

By the time hundreds of Conway's investors gathered at the Sheraton Hotel in Palo Alto for the fund's second annual conference, in October 2000, another dozen Angel companies had pulled the plug. Several called to mind the Calvin and Hobbes cartoon in which Calvin, with a bursting water balloon in hand, says, "How can something seem so plausible at the time and so idiotic in retrospect?" Best-Self is a weight management site that provided weight-loss tips and offered users a personalized page to help them track their daily caloric intake. Yoursafety.com described itself as a "crime and security data aggregation site," an interesting-sounding venue so long as no one figured on getting rich off the idea. TradeInteriors.com was a company that imagined basing a business on the interior design portal it had created, and another company going out of business not long after it was started was Vetmedsupply.com, which sought to supply medical supplies via the Internet to the country's veterinarians.

Conway knew he was in for some grumbling at his annual meeting, especially once he shared the bad news that he suspected that as many as thirty Angel companies would go belly-up by year's end. That represented 15 percent of the portfolio. Conway's answer was to throw another huge party. Again he opened his home to his investors and portfolio CEOs, and this time he really turned out the stars.

"The plan was to deliver the bad news and then flip it right away and show them a really great time," Conway says. "I figured this would be a good time to leverage our contacts in the entertainment industry. We decided to really stack it."

———

Arnold Schwarzenegger donated another car, and Dana Carvey again agreed to run the celebrity auction. There was no Warren

Dulled this time, but the star quotient burned even brighter than it had in May. Goldie Hawn and Kurt Russell were there, as were Paula Abdul, Ben Affleck, and Matt Damon. The guest list also included ICM's Jeff Berg and Leonard Armato, both big-time agents to the stars; Kay Koplowitz, the former USA Network president; Esther Dyson; and Herb Allen. The many bartenders scattered around Conway's yard were still pouring $35 bottles of Stags' Leap Cabernet, and at night's end Lise Buyer, hanging around out front while the valets fetched people's cars, swears she counted five people on cell phones calling ahead so their private jets would be ready to leave by the time they reached the airport. Yet the party just wasn't the same. The mood was more somber, the crowd less high on its own fumes.

Shaq, Tiger, and Arnold had all indicated through their people that they might come, but at the last minute all three backed out. There was still enough Hollywood tinsel to get people excited about the mingling of the entertainment industry and the Valley, but at least a few people in attendance were struck more by the disconnect than the potential synergies between the two worlds. The wife of one mogul-in-waiting elbowed her spouse and exclaimed, "That's Paula Abdul," but he answered, "Who's Paula Abdul?" There was the Internet CEO working hard to deliver movies and TV over the Web whom Conway sat next to Ben Affleck—and the CEO had to ask someone for the name of his interesting dinner companion. Affleck walked around the yard with a cigarette dangling from his mouth in a part of the world where conspicuous smoking is about as welcome as slurs about someone's race.

If five months earlier Buffett's presence dominated the post-party buzz, this time it would be Affleck's five minutes at the microphone. In the weeks leading up to the October 2000 event, Affleck had graciously agreed to host a dinner as part of the charity auction. When it came time for people to bid on his item, Conway invited him on-stage "to excite the crowd." Prim Angel staffer Jane Rush described Affleck's talk as "rambling and very odd," a woman CEO deemed it "deeply offensive." Affleck began by promising that Matt Damon would be included in the package, but from there, says attendee Joe Beninato, "it got raunchier. He says, 'We'll throw in oral sex!' 'We'll shave Matt Damon's butt!' " For his part, Conway described Affleck as "very suggestive and very funny, but he certainly didn't say 'oral sex.' " Whatever precisely he said, several people described Carvey as wincing the more Affleck carried on. "At one point [Carvey] covered the mike and whispered something to Affleck," Beninato says. "I don't know what he said, but I assume it was something like, 'You're crossing a real line here.' " In the end, the Affleck-Damon dinner/butt shaving fetched $135,000.

Andreessen walked away with the keys to another of Schwarzenegger's cars, this time a 1934 Bentley he bought for $135,000, and Damon and Affleck paid $25,000 for a pitch dinner with Andreessen and Loudcloud co-founder Ben Horowitz. Yet this time Conway raised barely over $500,000, not even half what he had raised in May.

Earlier in the day, at a formal meeting for his investors, Conway had spoken about his new expectations in a market that he was regrettably calling a "return to sanity." He told his audience that he was done playing Mr. Nice Guy. He vowed to identify the losers and drop them from his field of vision, to allow himself more time to focus on those he considered winners. The goal, he told investors, was still a 5X return, or a $400,000 profit on a $100,000 investment. Many investors were relieved, if not elated, to hear Conway's reassuring words, but the fund's Internet impresarios exchanged wide-eyed glances. Later at the party they asked one another, What's up with that? During his presentation, Conway had flashed a slide that showed that one fifth of the portfolio companies were b-to-c's and one fifth b-to-b's. Media and music made up another tenth of the portfolio. That meant at least half his portfolio companies were in precisely those fields that the smart guys had declared DOA—and it wasn't as if the 10 percent invested in search companies, 7 percent in "e-marketing/e-mail" companies, or 6 percent in e-finance were looking much more promising. So they asked themselves: Doesn't Ron read the trades?

—

In the spring the bad news had still felt like a trickle. There had been the occasional report about a company shutting down its site or laying off a portion of its workforce, but there was always an explanation that allowed insiders to treat the news as an isolated event and not indicative of any wider trend. Boo.com, a fashion retailer that sold high-end clothes online, burned through $135 million in two years before going paws up in May 2000. But Boo was an industry joke. The London-based startup spent lavishly on everything from advertising to office furniture to worldwide travel even as it lost money on every sale. Toysmart.com shut its doors, but that, too, was easily explained: of course backers abandoned this site lagging in fourth place in the race among online toy retailers. Similarly, two other high-profile busts, Brandwise and HealthShop, were also-rans in very crowded fields.

By June, the Nasdaq was starting to creep back up; by midsummer, it had regained half its losses. Companies were again getting in queue in hopes of going public. The prevailing wisdom then held that the days of successful "story stocks"—stocks with a compelling idea but no short-term prospects of a profit—were over, but that the public's appetite for hot new issues was hardly sated. "The markets," the smart-guy investment bankers assured everybody, would "always reward strong companies." The pathologically optimistic saw silver linings everywhere. Sanity meant the headhunters could no longer demand twenty thousand options on top of the steep fees they charged to find top-level talent—and of course talent was easier to find. Even rents fell. The nerdy joke making the rounds then was that "p-to-p" was no longer shorthand for the kind of "peer-to-peer" technologies employed by a Napster but "path to profitability." So now everybody was a p-to-p.

Yet even these small helpings of good news were deceiving. The Nasdaq's bigger companies, such as Cisco, Intel, and Oracle, were fueling the summer 2000 resurgence, not the smaller Internet companies that Conway's startups tended to look upon as inspiration. A long list of Internet companies were down more than 90 percent from their highs despite the Nasdaq's summer rebound, and the technology-oriented companies that went public then tended to be involved in biotech or businesses well positioned to cash in on one of two suddenly hot areas, wireless (Internet access via cell phones) and optical networks. Generally, the venture capitalists sat on the sidelines; meantime, the startups in which they had invested frantically slashed their advertising and marketing budgets. "During the summer," says Ram Shriram, "people were frozen in a state of slow decision making, like they couldn't quite process what they were seeing."

By November, the drip-drip-drip of the bad news started to feel like a hard rain that very quickly turned into a downpour. That month the Internet consulting powerhouse MarchFirst laid off 1,000 employees, or 10 percent of its workforce, while Covad laid off 400 and iXL.com, another Internet consulting firm, laid off 850. Among the high-profile companies shutting their doors that month: Furniture.com, MotherNature.com (online beauty aids), Pets.com (of sock puppet fame), and Swoon.com and Phys.com, both run by Advance Publications, owner of the Condé Nast magazine chain. Nearly 6,000 Internet employees lost their jobs in October, according to the outplacement firm Challenger, Gray & Christmas, and another 8,800 lost their jobs in November, through either layoffs or shutdowns. December was worse still. In the month's first full week, more than three dozen Internet companies confirmed that they had laid off a combined 28,000 employees, according to *The Industry Standard*'s layoff tracker, and another thirty-plus laid off at least 3,000 employees the following week.

By year's end, the stock sensations of 1998 and 1999 were the dogs of 2000. In 1999, *Forbes* magazine had touted Priceline.com founder Jay Walker as a "new-age Edison" on its cover, but after trading at $94 a share as late as March 2000, shares in Priceline hovered at barely over $1 by year's end. That was still better than a long list of Internet stocks that were trading in the pennies, including Theglobe.com, which was trading at 12 cents a share at the close of the year, and also Drkoop.com, PlanetRx.com, E-Stamp, EMusic, and Webvan, which was trading at 34 cents a share. When a company's stock falls below $1 a share, it faces the possibility that it will be delisted. Based on that criterion, the *Standard*'s Cory Johnson found that more than 250 companies risked a delisting at the start of 2001. Ask Jeeves, the apple of Conway's eye for so long, wasn't facing delisting, but it was still down 98 percent from its high. The usually self-confident Conway chides himself for failing to "distribute" shares of Jeeves to his Angel-I investors before its great fall instead of holding on to them long after the SEC's "lock-up" period had expired. (Typically, pre-IPO investors are not permitted to sell any of their shares in a company until at least six months after the offering.) "I was convinced Jeeves could do no wrong," Conway says. Marimba, another of Conway's earliest hits, was trading at below $5 a share, down from a high of $66.

It wasn't just the overnight sensations like Jeeves or Marimba taking it on the chin. The Internet blue chips had also been hammered in the last nine months of 2000. AOL fell 54 percent for the year and Yahoo and Amazon.com, the first two pure-play Internet companies to star on Wall Street, also suffered disastrous years. Amazon fell 77 percent for the year (and shortly into the new year, shut down two distribution centers and laid off 1,450), and Yahoo fell 86 percent.

The Nasdaq closed out the year by falling 87 points, or 3 percent, on its final trading day—the ninety-fourth time that year, the *Times* reported, in which the Nasdaq fell 2 percent or more. That seemed an apt close to what was now officially the worst year in Nasdaq history.

There was bad news beneath the bad news. Technology and non-technology companies alike were spending less on advertising, online advertising especially, and spending less, too, experimenting with cutting-edge products and services. That meant fewer potential customers for Conway's portfolio companies, and also less revenue. A bear market also meant a grimmer outlook for Conway's M&A strategy. A year earlier, a Yahoo or a Microsoft (its stock fell 63 percent for the year) would spend a couple hundred million dollars buying a startup that developed a feature (free e-mail, an online calendar, a portfolio tracker) that the bigger company could then offer its customers. With Yahoo's currency inflated so high that it was trading at more than a thousand times annual revenues, and with a market cap standing at an unjustifiable $125 billion, issuing new stock to cover a $400 million purchase was generally regarded as no big deal. The stock of every shareholder would be diluted, but so slightly as to make no appreciable difference.

Yet with Yahoo's stock battered and its currency deflated, the company would need to issue far more shares to cover the same $400 million purchase. At the end of 2000, when its market cap was hovering at around $15 billion, a big-dollar purchase would have a far more noticeable impact on the bottom line. Yahoo's purchase of Four11, a Web-based e-mail service, for $85 million in stock the previous year was the equivalent of Yahoo spending $12 million after its stock market fall. If Yahoo paid $85 million for an Angel Investors company, that would typically represent a handsome return of maybe four to ten times Angel's investment, depending on how early Conway had gotten into the company. At $12 million, investors might earn twice their money on some deals, but they would break even or lose on others. Yet even a $12 million sale was a long shot. Wall Street was watching every publicly traded Internet company that much more closely, and every company was doing what it could to cut costs. Suddenly $12 million didn't seem a pittance but a serious expenditure against the bottom line.

Within the Valley's venture world the expression was "the walking dead"—companies that churn out a steady, reliable profit but have no prospects for ever going public and scant chance of ever being acquired. The Valley's venture capitalists and its most aggressive angels aren't in the business of funding companies that produce a tidy 20 percent profit a year. The cliché is that early-stage investing is a "home run" business in which its practitioners are interested only in those companies that have the potential to provide a huge payout, through either an IPO or a merger. Yet for the foreseeable future neither option was in the cards for any but the most extraordinary of technology startups. Meanwhile, until the markets rebounded, the only way for a company to stay alive was venture capital, but the VCs were suddenly reeling with self-doubt. "The venture capitalists are frozen in place, not knowing what to do next," Sanford Robertson, a local éminence grise who was one of the first bankers to specialize in high tech, said shortly into 2001. Collectively, the VCs were sitting on tens of billions of dollars, but most were suddenly reluctant to part with a dime.

Even those companies that managed to go public were proving a disappointment. One Angel-II company, Loudeye.com, had gotten in just under the wire, going public in March 2000, and a second, AvantGo, dared the public markets that summer—and in short order both proved big losers. Conway had gotten into both deals at the height of the frenzy, and then only after their valuations had been inflated beyond reason. Loudeye was a D-round investment based on a valuation exceeding $150 million. It had cost Angel Investors $6.37 a share to get into the deal when Loudeye was still privately held; with Loudeye trading at $2 a share, in the spring of 2001, the $500,000 Angel Investors had invested in the company was worth only $162,000. Similarly, Angel-II didn't get into AvantGo until a D round held in April 2000 (Angel-I had made a C-round investment), and its investment was based on a valuation of roughly $250 million. Conway had gotten Angel Investors into AvantGo at $8.36 a share, when the company was still private, yet shortly into 2001 it was trading at $4 a share.

"I think we all had in the back of our minds that the dot-com craze couldn't last, that some of the air would go out of it. But nothing like the absolute collapse we've seen," says Joe Beninato, who had sold When.com to AOL for a price in the hundreds of millions in 1999. "We're talking about the highest of the highs and the lowest of the lows—in a single year." By the start of 2001, the same man-child CEOs who only one year earlier could do no wrong had suddenly fallen from favor. "I don't think venture capitalists want to be seen talking to me, at least in public," I-drive.com's Jeff Bonforte said in March 2001. "God forbid another VC would see us and say,

'Look, he's talking to a young, twentysomething entrepreneur. Didn't learn his lesson.' " Just as an overly forgiving market had allowed too many half-baked companies go public in the latter half of the 1990s, the new, more sober climate would probably be unforgiving the other way. "There are a lot of babies that will be thrown out with this murky bathwater," said venture capitalist Ben Dubin, a general partner with Asset Management.

"I think Ron played it right, but everything changed around him," Beninato says. "I think he needed another year of the highs to really hit it big. The hope now is that he'll get two or three huge hits that will make up for all the others." Beninato declines to predict what he thinks will happen, but he declares the "dot-com heydays" of 1998 and 1999 "something we'll never see again"—a statement that, if true, doesn't bode well for Angel Investors.

—

A year ago VentureWire, which tracks deals inside the venture capital world, was the best way for Conway's investors to follow the progress of their Angel portfolio companies. By the end of 2000, however, they'd have more luck reading about one of their investments in the *Standard*'s Layoff or Flop Trackers, if not a site called Fucked Company. If E-Trade and its promise of instant riches captured the zeitgeist in 1999, then Fucked Company's hand-rubbing glee over the carnage seemed to sum up 2000.

Fucked Company started as a one-time joke. The Nasdaq had already suffered its 34 percent drop when a twenty-four-year-old Web designer named Philip Kaplan spent part of Memorial Day weekend messing around with a spoof of a magazine called *Fast Company,* a bible for those who had embraced the fast-paced, the-only-rule-is-there-are-no-rules mind-set of the New Economy. Where inside the pages of *Fast Company* the pretty-boy twenty-eight-year-old wunderkind running a billion-dollar company is king, in Kaplan's creation he was fodder for a morbidly fun game that one might call a dot-com death pool. For kicks he imagined an online version of one of those celebrity death pools in which people bet on the famous people they think will die that year (you get more points for the twenty-seven-year-old rumored to be a speed freak than the octogenarian '40s-era film star). But within the world of Fucked Company, people would bet on terminal Internet companies. Kaplan e-mailed his spoof to a few friends and then hopped on a plane for Brazil. By the time he returned, at least the way the story is told, twenty thousand people had signed up to play. By the start of 2001, he was receiving a few hundred thousand page hits a month, and Kaplan, who goes by the nickname "Pud" (a bully's derogatory nickname for him when he was younger), had become one of the Internet's newest stars. When in February 2001 he posed for Women.com's "Men of the Internet 2001," he won.

On the surface Fucked Company seems wickedly good-natured, a slightly ghoulish way to have fun at the expense of people taken by their own invincible greatness. But click on the site's "Happy Fun Slander Corner" and you're assaulted by the stench of ignorance and cruelty. Anyone can send in an anonymous e-mail that is immediately posted to the site, but there's nothing cool about the site's vox populi nature. In mid-December, Bigstep (formerly the Springfield Project) laid off roughly one fifth of its staff, including two founders. People ridiculed the company's business model and offered that they were having a hard time mustering much sympathy for people who had been working so insanely hard to become new-Beemer rich. Fair enough, even if no one had cashed out yet at Bigstep, which was still a privately held company. But quickly it descended into a pool of nastiness. Scrotum, anus, cunt, sphincter, pussy—these ranked high among the more frequently used epithets on Fucked Company. It was like a giant room set aside for online adolescents looking to collectively jerk off.

Conway's portfolio companies gave Pud and his band of followers plenty of fodder. As Conway had predicted, thirty of his companies had shut down by year's end; six weeks into the new year, a total of forty-three Angel companies had gone out of business, representing a combined $22 million worth of investments. The dearly departed included the site that paid people to read ads, AllAdvantage, and also Candybarrel and Shaq's Dunk.net. Angel Investors also lost the $1.3 million Conway had invested in eRugGallery, and the $500,000 he invested in both ThatGlow.com, a "lifestyle Internet retailer" for pregnant women, and MoveSite.com, a "free, web-enabled move-management service to the corporate employee base" that described itself as a "b-to-e."

—

"When he commits to you," Artie Wu says, "he commits to you and your idea completely. You get the impression he'll do anything he can to help you." Yet that was easy for Wu to say as one of the chosen. Others had been secretly placed on what Conway euphemistically calls his "passive list," a printout of the portfolio startups he deemed terminally ill and therefore no longer worth his attention. In some instances, entrepreneurs knew they were on this running list Conway dubbed a "time-management tool," but in many cases they did not. By the spring of 2001, Conway had written off nearly one hundred companies, or nearly half the portfolio, though at that point Angel-I was barely two years old. The typical venture fund sees one third of its companies go out of business, and that's over a much longer time frame.

Conway & Co. tried valiantly to fight the tide. In January 2001, the staff sent sets of cassette tapes to every surviving portfolio CEO. The tapes addressed a variety of topics, from brand building to better management of a company's hiring and firing processes. In February, they hosted a "Corporate Partners Day," in March they sent around notices advertising a "Mentor Mania" morning, but the event was canceled for lack of interest. After b-to-c fell out of favor, suddenly a larger percentage of Angel companies were now calling themselves b-to-b's. But the b-to-b field had also gone suddenly cold, so Conway and staff were on the phone with the relevant companies, trying to help them figure out how to repackage themselves as a p-to-p (peer-to-peer) or a wireless play or whatever was both hot and plausible. "We've always got at least ten percent of our portfolio figuring out how to reinvent themselves," Margot Hirsch says.

"He must work twenty five hours a day," says Jane Rush, who handled Conway's calendar before leaving the firm early in 2001. She would speak with him on the phone at eleven-thirty at night and then arrive at the office the next day to find a fax laying out all the things he had thought about since they last spoke. He was working at so tenacious a pace that Hirsch was worried about his health. "I've never met anyone as hardworking and driven and conscientious as Ron," she says. Bill Campbell blamed the pace on the responsibility his friend felt to the 550 people who had entrusted him with money. "Ron," Campbell says, "is not a man to take responsibility lightly."

The new year brought more bad news, not all of it from the public markets. As the one-year anniversary of the Nasdaq's great fall approached in March, the index commemorated the occasion by falling below 2,000. That represented more than a 60 percent decline in less than twelve months. More Internet companies shut their doors, and Cisco, Intel, AOL, and Amazon were among the big-boy companies announcing widespread layoffs. Closer to home, Napster was in the headlines over its legal battles with the recording industry and nothing being reported boded well for Conway's highest-profile investment. Early in 2000, Conway was crowing about gaining a piece of this Web-based music-swapping site just as its popularity began to soar. Then in July of that year, a federal judge ordered Napster to halt the trading of copyrighted songs. In March 2001, a federal appeals court modified the order but upheld the bulk of it, prompting many pundits to declare the company's legal woes its death knell. Suffice it to say, the $1.5 million Conway sank into this free service has gone largely to legal fees.

Another problem was the flagging spirits of the young founders and CEOs on whose backs the fate of the fund rested. They would go fishing on Sand Hill Road, but then after weeks of nothing but nibbles they wanted to give up. Or they would have what they thought was a solid deal, but it would fall through, "and they feel burnt so they don't want to fish anymore," Bozeman says. Spirits were broken, too, by what in Valleyspeak they call a "down round."

That's when a VC tells a CEO that if she wants the firm's $5 million, then she'll be giving the firm a fat 20 percent slice of the pie rather than crumbs because her company, which once had a post-money valuation of $80 million, is now going to be valued at $25 million. Conway had told them that the power had shifted back to the VCs, but hearing those words wasn't like experiencing the disappointment firsthand. It was hard enough to give up on their billion-dollar IPO dreams. Now they had to accept that valuations had fallen by roughly 75 percent across the board. Being an Internet CEO didn't seem fun anymore.

"I had one CEO ask me, 'What's my incentive here to work harder?' " says Mike Kerns, Angel Investors' baby-faced junior associate. "When you hear that you want to scream at them, 'How about success? How about your employees and your investors?' " Some CEOs, Kerns says, wow him with their smarts and drive. Others, however, leave him wondering how they ever got where they are. "I'm twenty-four years old and I'm having to tell them, 'Hey, you need to do these things or you're going out of business,' " he says.

In February 2001, Conway addressed a letter to his investors. "A belated 'Happy New Year'—even though there's not too much to be happy about if all you are looking at is Internet stocks!" he began. We still haven't hit bottom yet, he warned, and he predicted that the bodies would continue to pile up. There was still plenty of time for many more companies to serve as happy fun fodder for Pud and his gang at Fucked Company.

———

No matter how grim the news, few inside the Angel Investors family could imagine that Angel-II would actually *lose* money. *Losing* money seemed impossible, as inconceivable as Ron Conway adopting a give-up tone. Microsoft and Compaq had invested in the fund. So had Esther Dyson and Ben Rosen, Sabeer Bhatia, Marc Andreessen, and Pierre Omidyar. Those weren't people who invested in losing funds, and Microsoft and Compaq didn't get to the top making dumb investments. For years the venture capital side funds

were reputed to be a guaranteed way to turn $1 million into $10 mil
lion. People adjusted their expectations based on the market's fall,
but instead of the 10X they had been expecting they figured they'd
earn three or four times their money. "Things have returned to nor-
mal," Beninato says. "The days when a side fund or a fund like
Ron's returns 10X are over." Beninato was among those predicting
that instead he might get a 3X or 4X return.

John Doerr had famously described the period that began in 1995
with the Netscape IPO as "the single greatest legal creation of
wealth in the history of the planet." The statement perfectly captures
the hubris of Valley culture. We don't just celebrate ourselves as the
king of kings at the center of today's world, we celebrate ourselves
as the king of all kings stacked up against any conceivable civiliza-
tion that's ever come before ours. Any culture that could embrace
Doerr's statement as its unofficial motto, as the Valley has done,
would find it hard to completely let go of the fairy tale. The have-
everythings could get their heads around elements of the new reality, but they couldn't quite embrace the whole thing. The Nasdaq
had fallen by more than half and profitless companies would no
longer be worth $2 billion in the blink of an eye, but it couldn't have
fallen apart that fast, could it? Typical was the view expressed by
Margot Hirsch: "I'm sure the fund will do fine," she said in January
2001. "It's just going to take longer than we originally thought to
show a return."

"There are a lot of people who treated all these side investments
as a guaranteed gravy train who are going to be very surprised," says
Paul Saffo, who in twenty years as a Valley denizen has witnessed
both the boom and the bust cycles. "People lose money when they
invest in the VC side funds. It's happened in the past and this is a
moment in time when you're going to see it happen again. Everyone
is just holding their breath waiting for the first fund to go bust."
Saffo says he doesn't have enough information to judge Conway's
fund, but he says that he "wouldn't be terribly surprised" if it ended
up returning less than 1X.

Conway was standing by his 5X prediction as late as March 2001. In his February "Dear Investor" letter, he had reported that the " 'winners' in our portfolio are continuing to show excellent progress." Conway's "winners" list included Napster and 12 Entrepreneuring, a company that Bozeman had described as "a company in serious trouble" in no small part, he said, because the two founders were no longer talking with each other. Just prior to sending out the letter, Conway had recalculated the numbers on Angel-II. He placed a zero next to those companies that had gone out of business, and he lowered the value of Angel's shares in any startup that had experienced a down round. Factoring in the handful of companies that had been bought and two that had gone public, the fund's assets were already worth, at $124 million, slightly more than the $121 million invested by that point. Officially, he said, "it is still way too early to predict the final outcome," but by those calculations, he proudly announced, Angel-II was already "above water."

The question, though, was how long Angel-II could continue to tread water. For one thing, there were all those companies on Conway's "passive" list, technically alive but representing another $20 million in bum Angel-II investments. For another, there were all those other shoes waiting to drop. Many of the companies on Angel-II's ledger sheet hadn't gone through a new round of financing; these were still being valued using prices dating back to a bygone era. Some would go out of business and be worth nothing; others would be lucky to sell for dimes on the dollar. After Conway had already done his calculations, the online invitation company Evite was sold. Evite had been valued at $102 million, according to the Angel-II ledger sheet, but the company was sold for roughly $20 million. Still others would go public but, like Loudeye and AvantGo, still might prove unprofitable, at least in the short run.

Not long after Conway sent out his February letter, Loudcloud became the third Angel-II company to go public. Loudcloud is Andreessen's company, an Internet consulting firm that seeks to take care of Web hosting for the world's largest companies. Just eighteen months earlier, when Andreessen and three cohorts founded the company, Loudcloud was about as hot a deal as the Valley had ever seen. When people were asked about the prospects for Angel-II, invariably they mentioned Loudcloud. Conway and Bozeman did, as did Jane Rush, Margot Hirsch, Donna Sokolsky, and Jennifer Bailey, among others. "Ron gets in when it costs pennies a share," Sokolsky explained. "Theoretically you only need a few hits to get a great return on the money. All he needs is two or three more Loudclouds."

Actually, one Loudcloud might prove one too many. Conway didn't exactly get into Loudcloud for pennies a share. All told, he invested $3.125 million from the Angel-II kitty in Loudcloud. The first $125,000 was invested when the company was valued at around $50 million. The remaining $3 million, though, was invested when the company, though still privately held, was valued at $920 million. The company filed to go public in October 2000, a decision that suggested boldness but in reality was based on desperation; though the company had raised $120 million in the summer of 2000, it was on pace to run out of money not many months into 2001. Initially, the company set a price that would have given it a $1.3 billion valuation, but it pulled the IPO and the deal was re-priced. The company went public in early 2001 and within a week's time, its market value slipped below $400 million. That wasn't bad for a profitless Internet firm that might never post any earnings, but it meant Conway's original $3.125 million investment was worth maybe $1.5 million. Rather than a hit, Loudcloud was heralded as proof the markets were still hostile to anything Internet-related.

Jennifer Bailey acknowledged that there's a chance that she and her husband might end up losing on their Angel investment, though she quickly added that she fully expects the Internet sector to rebound. Lise Buyer was not so sanguine. She said that it would be "great to get my money back," and then strode safely to the middle by declaring there was a chance she'd do better than that but there was also a chance she might not. A few of the jittery-smart investors in their twenties wondered aloud if their precious invitation into this most exclusive of funds might have been a privilege they could have done without, but they were careful to go off the record before sharing that view.

Most, however, grew philosophical when pressed about their expectations for the fund. Yes, she's worried, Jane Rush confessed, "but that's a decision I made back when I invested." Similarly, Donna Sokolsky allowed there's a chance she'll be "disappointed" by the return paid to her on her Angel investments, but she's adjusted by shifting to a five-year horizon. "You go into it knowing this is a risky investment," she says. Sure, the times look bleak, but that's why she's happy it's Ron Conway at the helm and not someone else.

In Ron We Trust: "If anyone can pull it off," Sokolsky says, "Ron can."

Chapter 7

—

FALLEN ANGEL

On the second Monday in March 2001, the Nasdaq fell below the 2,000-point barrier. The last time the index had been that low was December 1998, shortly after Theglobe.com had gone public and helped to spark the Internet mania that produced Angel Investors. It was in December 1998 that Conway asked a lawyer-friend to draw up the legal papers to create Angel-I.

Two days before that Monday in 2001 when the Nasdaq would fall below the 2,000-point plateau for the first time in twenty-eight months, Conway joined more than one thousand people at the Bay Meadows racetrack, twenty minutes south of San Francisco, for a glitzy Saturday night fundraiser dubbed "Denim to Diamonds." The event is sponsored each year by the Ronald McDonald House at Stanford, which provides a home away from home to the families of children receiving treatment for life-threatening illnesses at a nearby children's hospital. If there is one cause above all others with which Conway is connected, it's Ronald McDonald House, an organization he has served since the 1980s. It was Conway who fourteen years earlier had founded the Denim to Diamonds event, and he still stands as the organization's most effective fundraiser. He's one of the event's largest sponsors, and no one ropes in more wealthy donors than Conway. "He's our angel," says Alan Beach, the charity's director of development.

When Conway accepts someone into his network, he embraces that person as a full member in high standing. So when I asked Conway whom I should contact about attending the upcoming Denim to Diamonds bash, he told me he would take care of everything. He and his wife had already purchased fifteen tables at the event—no one else had bought even half that many, including Kohlberg Kravis Roberts & Co., the infamous investment house that was co-sponsoring the event. It would be silly of you to pay, he told me. I was curious to observe Conway in his social milieu, but I was receiving my first lesson weeks before the event was even to take place. The invitation I would receive by electronic mail described the night as a "black tie and glitzy Western evening."

At the previous year's Denim to Diamonds, with the Nasdaq a few days shy of its peak, Conway had entertained a crowd of partygoers by playing the part of a hapless blackjack dealer at the casino fundraiser that followed dinner. The moment served as a perfect metaphor for a short-lived era that was about to come to a close. "Ron was playing it straight, dealing as a dealer would deal—except he would keep hitting until he [went] bust. Every single time," says Octopus CEO Steve Douty, a social friend of Conway's. "There was this whole crowd of people who had gathered around, and everyone was betting everything they had and they wouldn't take any cards no matter what they had in their hands. And there'd be Ron, slapping down cards in this manic state: 'Shoot, a thirty-six.' People would be roaring with laughter as he gave them all their chips."

The 2001 event began with a two-hour champagne reception featuring a thirty-minute auction. The items auctioned off by news anchors from two local TV stations included a private cocktail reception for twenty at Giorgio Armani's San Francisco store and a week at Paris's Hôtel Prince de Galles. The Laurent-Perrier champagne was free, or you could pay $50 for one of four hundred

glasses that held the same beverage along with a gem. All but one of
the four hundred glasses had a cubic zirconium sitting at the bottom.
One contained a 1.6-carat diamond worth over $16,000.

As usual, Conway and his wife were late. Meanwhile, I spoke
with one of his sons, who had flown up from UCLA for the weekend. He told me about his father joining him, his friends, and other
dads on an annual fishing trip in Montana, and he laughed when I
said I couldn't picture his father in a setting that serene. "He talks
the whole time," Danny Conway told me. "I don't know if my dad
can keep quiet for more than five minutes." His parents arrived a little after seven-thirty. They were barely into the room before people
began to rush up to greet Conway; a steady procession of people
walked over to hover in his general vicinity, awaiting an opportune
moment to cut in. The ballroomlike hall in which the champagne reception took place was vast, running much of the length of the horse
track, yet in nearly an hour's time Conway never got more than
twenty feet into the room. His kingdom might be in tatters, but he
was still emperor in his little corner of the world.

The event was more subdued than in previous years. Attendance
was down slightly, and the organization's benefactors were not quite
as generous as they had been in recent years. Where in 2000 someone had paid $10,000 for the Armani cocktail party for twenty, in
2001 the high bid was $4,000. Conway again took a turn as a
celebrity blackjack dealer, but the crowd was not as jocular as it had
been the year before. The party was over, but of course the party was
hardly over for people such as Conway, who was still worth in the
tens of millions of dollars no matter how much money he had lost in
the previous twelve months. Only a tiny fraction of the money he
had invested in startups over the previous two years was his own—
and, in a way, he'd return to himself the money he had invested in
the fund (and then some) in the form of the ample salary he drew as
an Angel Investors general partner. He didn't pay himself $1 million
a year, the going rate among the general partners at the big venture
firms, but he compensated himself in the hundreds of thousands a
year. And, of course, he had been playing primarily with other peo-

ple's money. That's the magic of being a venture capitalist. There's no cap on the "carry"—the 20 to 30 percent cut of the profits that the general partners share—but they can't lose anything beyond the 1 percent of the total they customarily ante up when assembling a new fund. Even Bozeman, who at the start of 1999 had signed a $500,000 promissory note, was granted a reprieve. In March, two years after he signed the note, the partnership's lawyer nixed the arrangement, so Bozeman was no longer on the hook for half a million dollars.

When I spoke to him again shortly after Denim to Diamonds, Conway was still expressing confidence that Angel Investors would fare just fine. So many people had been chastened by all that had occurred in the previous twelve months, but not Conway. Maybe it was all those years in sales, where an unshakable belief in your product is key to both survival and success. ("Salesmen," cracked one Conway acquaintance, "always land on their feet, no matter how you throw them.")

Yet in short order reality would catch up with Conway. In early May, with the Nasdaq still hovering around the 2,000 mark, I asked him again if he was still optimistic about Angel Investors. "At this point, I'd be happy if I was able to get people their money back," Conway said. "And it's going to take a lot of work just to do that." He offered this confession in a glum voice I barely recognized. When I asked him what had changed, he was incredulous. "Look at what's happening in the markets!" he cried, as if admonishing me to finally take my head out of the sand.

Acknowledgments

Thank you to all those who agreed to talk with me for this work, starting with Ron Conway, who always proved frank and forthcoming and who generously allowed me to impose on his already overcommitted work life. Thanks to Bob Bozeman and the rest of the Angel Investors staff for their patience and time, and thanks, too, to a long list of people who are part of the wider Angel Investors family.

I am indebted to those who read a draft version of this work, despite a preposterously short turnaround time, including John Raeside, Randy Stross, Dashka Slater, Paul Saffo, and Jessica Barrows. Thanks go out to Bryan Shih, for his way with spreadsheets and valuations, and to my other valuable research assistant, who possessed a knack for seeing through the bull (and who sees the wisdom of remaining anonymous).

The Industry Standard was terrific about allowing me the time to work on this project; I couldn't have asked for a more supportive employer. Thanks to the *Standard*'s Jonathan Weber and the great team he's put together, and also thanks to my editor at Random House, Jonathan Karp, who was his usual persuasive and supportive self, and to my agent, Elizabeth Kaplan. Every author should have an agent like Elizabeth, wise, kind, and an impassioned advocate, and also a friend.

About the Author

GARY RIVLIN is the author of three acclaimed works of nonfiction, *The Plot to Get Bill Gates, Drive-By,* and *Fire on the Prairie: Chicago's Harold Washington and the Politics of Race,* winner of the Carl Sandburg Award for Nonfiction. His work has appeared in *Newsweek, The Washington Post, The New Republic,* and *The Nation,* among other publications. He is currently a senior writer for *The Industry Standard,* where he won the 2001 Gerald R. Loeb Award in the magazine category.

About AtRandom.com Books

AtRandom.com Books, a new imprint within the Random House Trade Group, is dedicated to publishing original books that harness the power of new technologies. Each title, commissioned expressly for this publishing program, will be offered simultaneously in various digital formats and as a trade paperback.

AtRandom.com books are designed to provide people with choices about their reading experience and the information they can obtain. They are aimed at communities of highly motivated readers who want immediate access to substantive and artful writing on the various subjects that fascinate them.

Our list features expert writing on health, business, technology, culture, entertainment, law, finance, and a variety of other topics. Whether written in a spirit of play, rigorous critique, or practical instruction, these books possess a vitality that new ways of publishing can aptly serve.

For information about AtRandom.com Books and to sign up for our e-newsletters, visit www.atrandom.com.

Printed in the United States
by Baker & Taylor Publisher Services